Create Your Business Plan for the Digital Age
Guide to an Effective Business Plan

Create Your Business Plan for the Digital Age

Guide to an Effective Business Plan

Humperdinck Jackman

TRANSNATIONAL PRESS LONDON

2021

Management Series: 10
Create Your Business Plan for the Digital Age - Guide to an Effective Business Plan
by Humperdinck Jackman

First Published in 2021 by TRANSNATIONAL PRESS LONDON in the United Kingdom, 13 Stamford Place, Sale, M33 3BT, UK.
www.tplondon.com

Paperback
ISBN: 978-1-80135-061-7
Digital
ISBN: 978-1-80135-062-4

Cover Design: Nihal Yazgan

Transnational Press London Ltd. is a company registered in England and Wales No. 8771684.

Table of Contents

2

About the Author

Humperdinck Jackman has thirty-year career of driving corporate growth in both the United Kingdom and the United States of America.

His career began with a privately funded venture in which he co-produced an original television series in California in the 1980's. A technology specialist, he transitioned into the software industry and took start-ups from concept through to listings on the London Stock Exchange.

An established Business Angel, among other ventures he is a Partner and Non-executive Director of Euro BPO Limited, a leading European-based staff outsourcing company.

A philanthropist, Humperdinck's most recent role was as founder and chairman of a British wildlife conservation charity to counter poaching in Africa.

His articles have appeared in The Times, The Telegraph, Audiophile Magazine, and Yachting Monthly among others.

Preface

As we approach 2022, there's never been a more promising array of opportunities for both business creation and expansion. The global marketplace is truly open: welcome to The Digital Age.

It's a time of profound change. Despite so many advances, e-Commerce and online marketing are reshaping the business world as we know it, and yet both are still in their infancy. Business must adapt or else risk stagnation and failure.

Napoleon mocked the United Kingdom as 'a nation of shopkeepers'. What of that nation today in which leading businesses sell physical goods without holding any inventory? Entrepreneurs are opening new enterprises without 'bricks-and-mortar' premises, while their back-office staff operate miles away. Innovation is the very root of growth, but it demands adaptive thinking – open minds – and plenty of imagination.

Whether you are planning a start-up or taking a mature business forward, crafting your business plan forces critical analysis. This, in turn, demands you justify your suppositions. It serves to eliminate the guesswork and to reduce risk. Above all, your business plan is not merely a tool for gaining investment but becomes, truly, your day-to-day survival handbook

How to Write a Modern Business Plan is a guide to encourage fresh thinking. It prompts the reader to leverage both technology and new business practises to forge a successful commercial destiny.

Shape your business for what you want it to become and be a business leader.

Humperdinck Jackman
London
July 2021

Part One
Designing your Business

Business Planning Fundamentals

- *Risk Awareness*
- *Finding New Ideas*
- *Analysing your Situation*
- *Using your Business Plan*
- *Defining your USP*
- *Your Elevator Pitch*
- *The Benefits of Mind Mapping*
- *The Benefits of Early SWOT Analysis*

Risk Awareness

Looking back forty years, the success and failure rates of new businesses remain remarkably steady, with the causes of both results remarkably unchanged. The current statistics for the United Kingdom are:

- 20% of new businesses fail in the 1st year
- 50% of new businesses fail within 5 years
- 6% of three-year-old businesses will fail in their next 6 months
- 5% of eight-year-old businesses will fail in their next 6 months

A survey of more than 100 failed large-scale start-ups revealed that a staggering 42% of founders declared the number one reason for failure was a marketplace which didn't want their product. A further revelation was that the next most common reason for failure is running out of cash (29%) followed by not having the right team (23%).

REASON FOR FAILURE

Not having
the right
team…

Product not
wanted
45%

Running out
of cash…

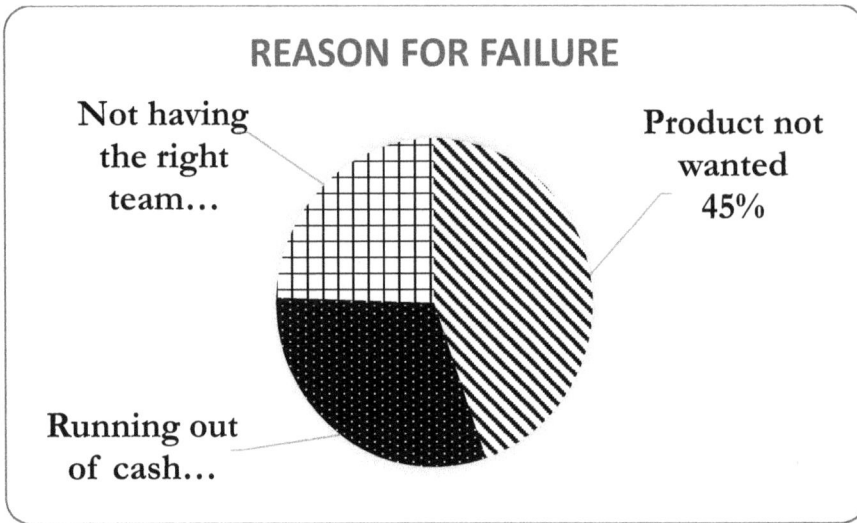

Being an entrepreneur should not be equated with being a gambler. Yes, there's a high degree of risk but in business, if you approach the process with care, the cards can be stacked in your favour. It's not luck: there is no house advantage, it just depends upon you.

> *Business Incubator or Accelerator Programs can increase SME success rates to a whopping 92%*

One of the surest ways to improve your chances of success is to kick-start your project under the auspices of a mentor. Business Incubator or Accelerator Programs can increase SME success rates to a whopping 92%, and that is surely worth considering. Apart from offering guidance across a myriad of topics, the best of such schemes facilitate introductions to customers, financiers, and specialist expertise perhaps far beyond your own.

A direct mentor, such as a Business Angel or Non-executive Director can work wonders for the newcomer. Apart from their own considerable experience, you will find they have a contact list which opens doors and solves problems in the blink of an eye.

Sole traders are also likely to fail. The 'right team' infers just that: not one person trying to do it all, no matter how ingenious or good of a leader. Two heads are always better than one, and even more so if from different backgrounds.

Good research is paramount. In 2014 the successful businessman and retail magnate Theo Paphitis, formally of the Dragons Den television series, was asked about the failure rate of small businesses and had this to offer:

> *"They haven't done the research; they don't know where to go for the right funding ... it's rarely one thing. The reason people fail is because they don't do their homework. You wouldn't sit an exam without doing any preparation. A business is no different. It's about knowing more than the next guy or girl and performing better, and the only way you can do that is through knowledge. It's basic stuff but we don't do it."*

Small and Medium-sized Enterprises (SME's) are critical to the economy. Fifty per cent of the UK's GDP comes from SME's, so it's clear that there is considerable success to be won. Equally certain is that your own due diligence is essential. Take off the rose-tinted glasses and look objectively at your idea: is it reliant on wishful thinking and luck? If you can't justify your plans, if you can't interest others to invest, then you should work on refining your approach or seek a new opportunity.

This brings us nicely to the use of business plans which you should think of not as some tedious questionnaire dumped upon you by your bank, but rather a valuable tool. Your plan will force you to appreciate risks, seek resolutions, create new ideas and approaches and, above all, it enhances your chances of success.

Take time over it, and never be shy about admitting to yourself that what seemed like a good idea was too filled with risk or uncertainty: just start over and develop something new. If you write ten business plans before settling on 'the one', then think how much money you saved by not spending anything but time on the turkeys.

Finding New Ideas

Are you just going to copy and enhance what's been done before? It's not a bad idea, especially if it falls within your areas of expertise and interest. Go through the entire process and explore ways and means to develop better approaches. These might include better customer service, more profitability, leveraging the internet or a myriad of other possibilities. Out of this you can create something special.

For many people, though, there's a yearning to branch out. This might include using one's skills in innovative ways, or abandoning the desk job for something healthier.

Others just reach a point where they realise that they hate their line of work and need change. Needing change isn't always enough: they need an income too.

Finding your niche isn't always so easy, though, so where are the fresh ideas?

Franchises

A good 'first step' is to explore the franchise marketplace, not just in your own country but overseas. Look across Europe, Australasia and the United States especially, as franchises which are proven in one locale are more likely to have a resonance in your own region. Asia, though, has many innovations and might trigger a thought worthy of exploration.

If indeed you decide to take up a franchise, apart from needing to satisfy the franchisee of your viability, be aware that you are often obliged to operate within a rigid corporate culture, where the structures limit your freedoms to innovate.

However, the franchise marketplace is also an opportunity to explore up and coming business concepts. If a group in California have a successful new approach to creating and marketing the latest fad – 'slimming smoothies' or whatever – then can you develop the same in your territory?

Going it alone means you will have to learn for yourself many of the mistakes that the franchisee made in the first place. However, you also have the flexibility to make modifications to the idea and, naturally, you don't have to pay someone for the privilege.

Blogs

With so many blogs being written to very high standards, following several which focus on aspects of your profession is an enjoyable way to gain inspiration. Many entrepreneurs detail their day-to-day challenges, with some even reporting their monthly revenues.

Engage with a writer you admire and explore their business models in a respectful fashion. The world is a big place, and there's always room for one more business.

Dare to branch out of your comfort zone and see what other people are doing to create new businesses. I do, however, find forums to be entirely too tedious and the ideas over-worked. For all of the time you must spend filtering through the 'noise', it's hard to access quality thought.

Online Magazines

There is a treasure trove of good information published in all manner of online magazines.

Many are written especially for the SME, and they offer a national or regional focus. Those run by local government business development agencies and business incubators represent a remarkable resource.

Apart from learning what ventures people are undertaking in any particular region, you will read of accessible financial assistance programs, access to expert advice and – possibly – even discover that there's a newly formed business which you might join.

The local area market research is often invaluable, including detail on demographics, disposable incomes, employment rates, facilities, and costs of conducting business within a region.

Business Angels

Sites which have an emphasis on Business Angels – smaller scale private investors – contain a veritable gold mine of ideas and inspiration.

You will read overview of all manner of business ideas, many backed up with summary business plans. Some will make you cringe and others will make you sit up and take notice.

One advantage of exploring these sites is that you get to put yourself in the shoes of investors. Very quickly you will be dismissing some proposals as un-researched nonsense. Ask yourself why you were so turned off. Was the idea too fanciful, or was the thinking akin to reverting back two decades?

These sites contain many business ideas from individuals seeking business partners. Perhaps one might be an ally for you? Be cautious, but with proper due diligence, why shouldn't you consider forging a relationship with a stranger seeking an active business partner?

Analysing your Situation

As one starts the process of writing a business plan, there's the excitement of knowing that you are crafting your destiny. It's liberating to consider the possibilities, but therein lies some risk: until this stage you have perhaps been wearing 'rose tinted glasses', and you may believe your concept is brilliant, unique, and a sure-fire winner. Perhaps it is, although it's unlikely to be all three. Now prove it!

The best business plans are those written by entrepreneurs who have forced themselves to approach the process with a degree of detachment. They use the plan as a tool for stimulating critical thinking, and it's out of this that fresh ideas are nourished.

At some point on this journey, you might see that a particular component of the business process is where the effort should be invested. Don't be afraid to change.

Rejecting your plan is also a success. Smile and start over. You didn't lose money!

Weigh every aspect of your proposal. Even after many weeks of research and analysis, if you recognise a lack of feasibility then rejecting your plan is also a success. Smile and start over. You didn't lose money! And since many start-ups seek investment or loans from friends and family, your reputation home and career remain intact.

There's no 'One Size Fits All' solution. Too many books and articles on business plans fail to recognise that there is no 'one size fits all' approach to crafting a business plan. There are, after all, three broad scenarios:

○ SME start-up. One to three partners, self-funded by cash, a line of credit or with personal loans from a bank, friends or family. With significant experience and reputation, they might be backed by a Business Angel or other investors.

○ Existing SME business. Has at least three years of audited accounts, a solid trading history and customer base. Typically, now reaching out for expansion funding from banks, venture capitalists and business angels.

○ Employer expansion. You are pitching a plan for your employer to expand or diversify and you (and your colleagues?) propose to make it succeed. You must gain the Board's endorsement and investment.

THE SMALL SIZED START-UP

The most common scenario and the one which carries the biggest risk. You have a lot to lose and everything to gain, and almost zero chance of securing a commercial bank loan. Depending on your location, though, there are numerous start-up 'Business Incubators', government grants and other useful schemes for which you may qualify.

In all likelihood you know your trade or industry and you're confident in your skills, or perhaps you are considering taking on a franchise operation?

Your access to assured funding will range significantly, but will typically lie in the region of £10,000 – £100,000. At the outset you will be reliant upon your own assets such as cash, an equity loan against your property, other investments or you might sell some assets to raise the cash. The objectives of your business plan are quite straightforward:

○ Critical analysis of the feasibility: can this work?

○ Attract a business partner to join your venture.

○ Secure some modest investment from friends and family?

○ Detail the resources required.

There's no absolute reason why you shouldn't be a sole trader, but there are countless advantages in sharing the burden with a partner. These include such aspects as sharing the workload, gaining motivation, halving the financial risk and, most importantly, doubling the rate at which potential clients may be reached.

> *Starting a business can be a lonely venture and two heads are generally better than one*

A partner brings a fresh perspective to problem solving which is an order of magnitude more complex and draining when you're on your own. Apart from saving you from working in isolation, having someone you trust and respect, and who is working to the same ends, can transform your sense of well-being. In other words, starting a business can be a lonely venture and two heads are generally better than one.

Don't overlook the financial advantage. Not only can a business partner doubling the available start-up finding, but they can also halve the financial risk. After all, if you are unsuccessful, will you have ruined your own financial situation? Would your home be at risk?

Your business will require a level of investment in tools of the trade, regardless of whether this might mean exactly that for the tradesman, but it's the same for the information technology business which requires computers and software licenses.

Business premises, transportation, marketing and many other overheads consume your budget with frightening speed, as do business licenses, insurance and third party professional services. Maximising your budget by selecting the most promising business model and embracing the digital economy is critical to success.

The best advice is to assume the plan will require fifty percent more funding that you anticipate at the outset.

THE MID-SIZED START-UP

For the sake of argument, let's assume the mid-size start-up has access to cash or credit in the range of £100,000 – £500,000. It's a huge spread indeed, but well within the norm. Frustratingly, you share the headache of the small-sized start-up above in that it is still relatively unlikely that any bank will grant a commercial business loan on any terms which aren't at punitive levels of interest. The substantial part of your funding will come from your own pockets.

> *These partners have considerable experience and reputation and within their industry …*

A new business with this capital is most likely to be formed by partners who have worked together within the industry, often for the same employer. Tired of the perceived limitations and frustrated by missed opportunities, they decide it's time to strike out independently. Another common denominator is that these partners have considerable experience and reputation within their industry. They know where to find the clients and probably have some 'waiting in the wings'.

While this potential business has no trading history, their reputation and networking connections often opens the door to interest from a Business Angel or Venture Capital operation. Their business plan will feature additional elements:

O Considerable emphasis on research, solid financial projections and access to beneficial supplier terms.

O Backed by a sophisticated marketing plan

O Credible enough to attract investment from experts

O Details of the professional services (accountant, bank, lawyer, insurers etc.) have already registered the company, domain name, trademarks,

Such a business plan is created in stages. The founding partners create the framework and flesh out the financials just as the smallest business. Once convinced that the plan has merit they might then seek additional business partners and make the appropriate registrations. This is important if one wants to attract a professional investor and it makes the business plan significantly more professional and enticing.

They will certainly go one step further: their market testing will seek out clients who will bring business from the outset. This is a complex process and one which causes many legal problems with current employers if not handled ethically. Suffice it to say within the scope of this book, the probability of success multiplies drastically if one can go to market with clients on board.

With considerable money at stake, the legal costs involved are worth the pain. The requirement for a professionally drafted Shareholders' Agreement (SHA) is an absolute. This legal contract structures the relationship between shareholders of a business. It provides the legal basis as to how the owners of the corporation shall interact with each other and with the directors. Note, that the shareholders and the directors may be one and the same.

> *Without a shareholders' agreement your investment may disappear in legal fees.*

The SHA will govern dispute resolution and, with goodwill, may avoid costly legal battles in the future. Relationships do become strained and there's nothing like money to ruin a friendship. While you and your partners may be best friends, what happens if one partner falls sick for an extended time? What happens if one partner dies? What if one partner feels as if they are generating all of the revenue and the other isn't pulling their weight? Without a shareholders' agreement your investment might disappear in legal fees.

THE EXISTING BUSINESS

The directors of a business with three or more years of trading history have the cards stacked in their favour. They survived. They've forged their niche and gained a client list after all of their hard work and diligence. Perhaps now they are making a modest profit while paying themselves a respectable salary. Hopefully the business has adequate cash in the bank to ride the downturns and finance the upturns. Debtor days are down, and they look forward with optimism.

At this stage, the directors might be acknowledging that if they had x more resource they could achieve y more revenue and so this new business plan might be a radical revision of their initial objectives: a shake-up of how they approach the marketplace, or a fundamental shift in direction in response to market forces. With their track record and proven ability as evidenced by their audited accounts, it's time for them to approach the financial institutions and other sources of funding to facilitate expansion way beyond their own capacity.

Characteristics of the business plan for the existing business are much the same as for the Mid-Sized Start-up but with heavy emphasis on the following:

O Explaining why and how your leadership delivered growth

O Extreme emphasis on the credibility of the financials

O Assurance that the growth to come is of minimal risk

O Attractive growth rates (> +25% – 50% p.a.) for the future

O Strategy for next three years

O Fresh ideas and how and why these will contribute to growth

O Why an investment in this company is a low risk proposition?

O The Return on Investment (ROI) and the Exit Strategy

Specialist advice is now the order of the day, and you should consider the skills and capabilities of all of your professional service advisers. Are they the best informed? Are they willing and able to contribute to the final reviews of your new business plan and make it the most credible possible? Especially at this transitional stage of the business, which you have fought so hard to create, you can't afford second best.

> *Now is the time to find the best firm of accountants you can afford.*

In the early days, when every expenditure was agony, your choice of accountant was simpler: you wanted to keep the tax office off of your back and let you focus on business. Now is the time to find the best firm of accountants you can afford. They will be aware of new opportunities, such as superb government backed investment schemes which generate massive tax relief for both the directors and other shareholders, or perhaps you will be advised of how to invest in the business at preferential rates.

EMPLOYER EXPANSION

Whether one is working for an SME or a multi-national corporation, there often comes a time when it's either part of one's job to create a new business plan for a department, the business overall or for one's own ambition.

Your advantages are numerous, insofar as you are a known quantity, your abilities are respected and you have an intimate understanding of the business. This very familiarity tends to be the undoing of many, since the business plan is too casual, too lacking in substance.

While following the overall concepts of the three scenarios above, they are all valid, when creating a business plan for one's own employer consider the following:

O Have you been tasked with this objective? If not, will your employer take this as a sign that you are dissatisfied?

O Is the plan fully complimentary to the employer's business model?

O Have you researched your employer's financial situation? Is there cash in the bank? Is the business profitable?

O Is the financial investment proportionate to the business' size?

O Will your plan increase profitability? How? By how much? When?

O Is there anything in your plan which could be misconstrued as saying 'you know better than the boss'?

O Is change welcome?

O If your plan is rejected, how will you feel?

If you are writing such a business plan to fund what, in effect, will become your own business entity, then ask yourself if you are not just treating your employer as a bank?

Sometimes it's better to strike out on your own and 'plough your own furrow'.

Consider if you have the assets to head out independently? Sometimes it's better to strike out on your own and 'plough your own furrow'. Independence doesn't mean you cannot maintain a cooperative and close relationship with your employer, but it can mean that the hard work will pay increased dividends to you.

Other Considerations

Your business plan is far more than a document to be trotted out to banks and financiers in general. It's your own sanity check, and the primary means you will have to manage both yourself and your business operations.

As professor of entrepreneurship, William B. Gartner of Clemson University in the United States says 'business plans are essential', and the U.S. Small Business Administration (SBA) echoes the same, 'The importance of a comprehensive, thoughtful business plan cannot be over-emphasized.'

TIME

While it is true that some opportunities have a very short window of engagement, such as being offered a specific business for sale, your plan is surely to remain in business for five years or longer. With this in mind, don't rush! The more you contemplate the business concept and examine the pros and cons, the less likely you are to make a fundamental mistake which could lead to losses or even failure down the road.

MONEY

Be honest with yourself and consider the required start-up costs. Most new businesses require considerably more cash than owners anticipate, all the more so if starting a business from the ground up rather than buying an existing concern.

Do you have your own cash or any potential financial backers? How is your credit, and are there any black marks? Are you eligible for grants or other assistance from government agencies?

As you develop your business plan, it is well worth reaching out to your network of family, friends, industry associates and others to gauge the viability of how you will fund the new enterprise.

EXPERTISE

Are you an expert in your field? Do you have the knowledge and skill set required to increase the likelihood of success? Consider this early in the process and either delay your plan or seek one or more partners with the particular experience you require.

For some ventures, it might be that a training course give you the boost you need, and for others an additional qualification is often available.

RISK TOLERANCE

Are you financially secure, or would failure of your enterprise cause significant damage to your career, lifestyle, family, or relationships? How can you mitigate these risks, and how could you approach your planning to minimise the risks?

There is nothing wrong in realising that a particular idea is too risky. If you are to succeed, you cannot spend your days metaphorically 'looking over your shoulder' in fear of failure.

FINANCIAL RETURN

The harsh reality of business is that rarely is there profit in the first year, and if starting a particularly small venture it might be a struggle to extract much cash at all in the form of a salary or dividends.

Consider your cost of living, and factor in any mortgages, car payments and other fixed overheads. Do you have a spouse or dependent children? Are you willing to reduce your outgoings and, if so, how?

Whether your venture will launch with just yourself and a partner, or whether there will be a staff of ten, your income is likely to suffer for a while. Ensure you can ride it out until the business can start to pay you what you require.

ENJOYMENT & FAMILY

Commitment is key, and with this comes the certainty of long hours and minimal free time. Your business will own you, and it's not uncommon for the entrepreneur to work seven days a week and to consume all of one's waking hours. Vacations become unaffordable luxuries, not because of money, perhaps, but because you will probably lack the resources to not be there for your clients.

You probably have the stamina, but how about those around you? Tensions form in relationships when one person is committed to a business at the cost of spending enough time on the relationship itself.

PROFESSIONAL GUIDANCE

Now is the time to connect with the people you already know, people who have started businesses, and perhaps you know a lawyer, accountant or other specialist? Seek friendly advice and accept input and opinion.

At some point, though, you are well advised to pay for professional independent counsel. You will need a lawyer, accountant, banker, insurance broker and much more. For the start-up, these services are often available through government agencies or even a High Street bank, but remember that quality often comes at a price.

Using your Business Plan

You may or may not be an expert in your field, just as you may or may not have ever run a business. Nonetheless, even experts in their fields who are self-funding require a business plan.

You might have a nice nest-egg of savings, equity in your home and so forth, but very often the self-funded business person is also using loans or investment from friends and family. You owe it to them to complete your due diligence and, for this, the business plan becomes your set of tools.

Your Business Plan is a 'Live' Document

Until the day on which you close, sell, or retire the business, your business plan is never finished. To say it's finished is akin to saying that you've run out of ideas.

regard your business and marketing plans always as 'works in progress'

You might be happy with things as they are, but your competition is always nipping at your heels, whether you are aware of them or not.

Other factors, such as changing taxation and employment law, need periodic revision in order that you manage risks and plan for changes to your required expenditures.

You must regard your business and marketing plans as 'works in progress', constantly updating according to the business climate.

Set dates for quarterly reviews with your business partners and, perhaps, key employees, and measure success against your goals. Naturally, you will be running such financial exercises on a monthly basis, but what of client acquisition? Client satisfaction? Achieving marketing milestones?

In the Digital Age, changes can be forced upon a business in days or weeks (sometimes even only hours), and it is only through anticipation and preparation by which can assure our on-going success.

Basic Resource Planning Tool

It will help you see the resources required, and perhaps it will reveal that your initial location is not ideal, or that the talent pool you require is lacking. Never be afraid to turn the plan on its head and reassess even the most basic premise.

Professional Services Tool

How will you structure your business (what form shall the legal entity take) and how shall it be capitalised? As you develop your plan, it is quite likely that you will see value in bringing in a third party and so you are on the road to developing the 'right team'.

It follows that you might then require additional professional services, such as a solicitor to draw up a shareholding agreement.

Progress Evaluation Tool

You're going to be your own boss, and so your plan becomes your evaluator. By referring back to the final business plan you can monitor your progress against your early goals and expectations.

If you are falling behind on any of the key metrics, then understand why and make the changes. Referencing your original plan and revising your direction can make all of the difference to your survival. This should be a process in which all Directors participate on a fixed monthly schedule.

You must hold yourself and your fellow directors accountable and signing off on a final published plan is a certain approach to ensuring you can do exactly that.

Recruiting Tool

In the early days especially, your business plan might be your best tool for recruiting staff. You want the very best you can afford, right? So the business plan provides your candidates with a sense of security: if your plan makes sense, and the prospect of career growth is realistic, then perhaps they will suffer a reduced income and accept the risk for the rewards which might follow.

Don't forget, for many people there is a strong preference towards being a big cog in a small wheel. Above all, if your staff feel fully vested in success because they understand – and believe in – the goals, then they are more likely to strive for success.

A positive reaction to your business plan by a candidate for employment is hugely beneficial. Does the potential accountant become enthusiastic at how the business is to be managed from a financial perspective? Does the potential salesperson get excited by the back office support, the commission structure and the product portfolio? Let them review your plan and listen to their reactions, ideas and grasp of what you are really trying to achieve.

It's hoped that you have some interesting ideas, and if you happen to add your proven track record in being successful, then you might find your costs of employment are greatly reduced and you start with the best possible staff.

As the business builds, it's these people who will thrive and who themselves will seek some co-ownership. At each stage, the business plan will serve to remind everyone of the core objectives.

Investor Tool

Any prudent investor will demand to review your business plan, although I've met a few who were exceptions to the rule. This process might require many meetings until agreement is reached and funds are released, and more than a few such discussions will be fruitless.

The experienced investor may be incredibly demanding. You must keep an open mind while refining the plan accordingly. I've rejected business plans because the projected growth rate is way beyond industry norms and are, magically, to be achieved with one third of the number of sales staff. Although just an oversight by the authors, the addition of the extra headcount did affect the entire set of financial projections quite drastically.

Above all, the business plan should be accurate and honest. But think, if that business had launched on a faulty premise, then what would have become of the principals and their own money?

Operational Planning Tool

From the day you open the doors for business, you will be adhering to an operational plan, in which you defined your sales, marketing, recruitment, financial, capital expenditure and other operational milestones.

Within your comprehensive business plan, you may, for example, have defined that the business must achieve 120 sales in its first year. You believe this is reasonable because you have industry experience.

With your operational planning tool, you are thus able to measure your progress towards this and take prompt action for shortcomings.

O   Did the sales people contact 120 potential customers this month?

O   Did they present the product to 60 customers?

O   Did they write sales quotations for 30 customers?

O   Did they get the 10 orders expected in the business plan?

You plan is thus your baseline. This is what you must measure yourselves against since you have no trading history and only your projections to determine progress, whether for better or worse.

Defining your USP

Understanding your USP, or Unique Selling Point, remains as valid a concept today as it did when first conceived in the early 1940's by Rosser Reeves of the United States television company Ted Bates & Company. What, it demands, is special about your product?

In an article which was published by the Harvard Business Review in 2011, it said 'Differentiation is one of the most important strategic and tactical activities in which companies must constantly engage.'

Dominos Pizza created a perfect example in 1973 with their mantra, *'You get fresh, hot pizza delivered to your door in 30 minutes or less – or it's free.'* There was no doubt in the mind of the customers as to what this meant and the clear benefit. Their sales exploded.

Product positioning, gaining 'mindshare' and such terms are derivatives of the USP model. The focus is upon creating a perception in the mind of the customer that when they see your product or brand or trademark that they form a cognitive association which is stronger than that of your competition. Think of Ronseal, the wood preservative: *'It does exactly what it says on the tin'*, and this is understood by the population at large, regardless whether they've ever had a wooden shed or fence to treat with such a product. Twenty-two years later and that slogan is still being used with success.

So what's yours? What makes your idea so special?

○ Is your product or service truly innovative?

○ Can you fulfil a need which has been overlooked?

○ Do you save your client money vs. the competition?

○ Is your product styling the differentiator?

○ Is it you and your reputation?

○ Is your product tastier, fresher, faster, friendlier, larger or smaller?

○ Is your product more efficient, 'greener', more varied?

Spend time on this. When it comes to creating your marketing plan or enticing an investor to accept that your business plan is the one to trust, this is certainly one of the most compelling factors.

Remember too, that 42% of CEO's of new SME's which later failed cited that the market didn't want or weren't ready for their product offering. Face it, if you can't convince yourself then how will you convince your customers?

For now, create a list.

The Elevator Pitch

A much-overlooked concept remains a critical one: how do you interest someone in your product or service quickly, concisely and in such a fashion that they might be intrigued enough to wish to know more?

Ilene Rosenzweig and Michael Caruso, an editor for Vanity Fair magazine coined the term, 'The Elevator Pitch'. They realised that they might bump into a senior executive on the elevator and have up to thirty seconds with a captive audience, a unique window of opportunity to engage and win them over with a unique proposition.

> *"The purpose of an elevator pitch is to describe a situation or solution so compelling that the person you're with wants to hear more even after the elevator ride is over." – Seth Godin*

If perfected, one hoped to step out of the elevator and continue talking to his new contact in the hallway, and so begin a new opportunity or, at the least, the exchange of business cards.

The key is not to be too specific but, rather, to entice your listener to become curious. For example, in response to '*Why are you here? What do you do?*', there's nothing to be gained in answering with, '*I sell photocopiers for XYZ Inc.*'. Far more engaging might be '*I'm here working with Mr. Bloggs to explain how our technology can reduce his departmental costs by 40% this year*'.

Oh really? Tell me more!

When employees are interviewed, the consensus among psychologists is that the hire / don't hire decision is often made within the first seven seconds. Regardless of whether you will end up standing in front of a venture capitalist or your father-in-law, and you are seeking funding, you must be ready. Your business plan and later sales success depends on this because many of your customers are going to be equally demanding,

Imagine someone planning to open an upmarket coffee shop and revealing that this is why they are seeking £150,000 of funding. Their audience knows what a coffee shop is, they might know how profitable they can be, but *why is this particular coffee shop* venture so special as to deserve some consideration? How might this go?

The 12 Second Pitch

Summarise in one sentence exactly what you offer.

> *'We offer the freshest coffee in the United Kingdom'*

Describe the benefits that your product or service provides. List the features that set your product or service apart from your competitors' products or services.

'Our coffee is unique in several ways: it's grown by our own staff on a mountain in Ethiopia, we fly it in freshly each week and we roast the beans in-house according to each customer's own preference and we serve it in the true Ethiopian style. You've never experienced flavour quite like it ... have you tried it yet? Here's my card!'

The 30 Second Pitch

With thirty seconds you can be more descriptive. Use a few simple sentences to summarise your company's offering.

'We provide the finest coffee available in the United Kingdom. Our coffee is grown by us on a mountain in Ethiopia and we fly it in every week.'

Now explain what makes you so special. Try to include the major benefits of your product or service and list the most salient features.

'Our coffee is unique in several ways: it's grown by our own staff on a mountain in Ethiopia, we fly it in freshly each week and we roast the beans in-house according to each customer's own preference and we serve it in the true Ethiopian style. You've never experienced flavour quite like it ... have you tried it yet? '

'Coffee was discovered in Ethiopia and we realised that the way it's served delivers unmatched flavour. We also discovered that we can dispense with the expensive and noisy machines to prepare it. This makes for a more pleasant experience for the coffee devotee while helping the growers directly.

Now explain your company's qualifications:

'We've been in business for five years and we have won various awards'

Now describe your goals:

'We are planning to expand from two branches to ten within the next six months'

Okay, so the above is a fictitious example, but create your elevator pitch early and refine it as your progress. It will help to direct your thoughts and keep you on track.

The Three Minute Pitch

Work at your introduction so you can talk for up to three minutes, but don't rush it. Read the body language and be prepared to vary, curtail or get to the point, such as, 'Would you like to visit?'. You want to convey the following:

○ Who are we?

○ What we do

○ What makes us so special?

○ Why we will succeed?

○ Why you need us!

○ What would you like to know?

Regardless of whether you are offering computer programming or cups of coffee, your objective is to arouse curiosity and enthusiasm. Your audience should be intrigued and, thus, leave them opportunity to react with questions or requests. Above all, you are not trying to close a sale right now, you are piquing interest and – with luck – the chance for further discussion.

The Benefits of Mind Mapping

There's little doubt that it's a rare business these days which offers a unique product desired by everyone. It does happen, and for the lucky few the customers beat a path to the door. For the rest, though, it's a perpetual quest to grow the business amongst thriving and well-established competition.

Hard work and being a master of your craft are prerequisites, but if you add fresh thinking to the mix and, as the saying goes, you *'think outside the box'*, you stand a better chance of improving the odds and gaining an advantage.

When drafting your business plan, the technique of brainstorming and its digital companion, mind mapping, are second to none for unleashing your creativity.

A Fresh Approach to Old Problems

Adjusting your mind-set to be receptive to new ideas is an essential start, so throw away your rule book. Just because something has always been done one way, doesn't mean there's not a better alternative, especially when technological improvements are arriving ever faster. Indeed, the faster the pace of change, the more we need to unleash our imaginations and use all of the resources available to us to filter it and identify what can assist us and, equally, what represents mere distractions. The knowledge is there - we just have to access it.

> *the relatively simple process of naming your venture has become a headache thanks to computers and the internet*

Taking an obvious example, how might you come up with a unique company name in 2016? It's practically a given that you will want a website and thus it's not just a name and trademark you require but the requisite domain names too. You might register Business Guru Limited but what are the costs, perils and pitfalls if businessguru.com and businessguru.co.uk are both taken? Thus the relatively simple process of naming your venture - or product - has become a handsome headache thanks to the internet.

Until the advent of the global internet and thus the global marketplace, you might have engaged the services of a product naming company. Typically lawyers, their task is now far more complex and their invoices ever more substantial. Using Brainstorming you can help yourself to massive savings by doing so much of the grunt work yourself.

How does this work? Traditionally, you might sit with a friend or family member and toss out a few ideas. Then a work associate. Slowly you assemble some names but it takes time. In a brainstorming session, a small group of people use unstructured techniques for the rapid and spontaneous generation of ideas. Each member of the group creates new ideas by feeding off those already proffered. Originality is the result.

Used properly, Brainstorming and its modern derivative, Mind Mapping, are fun, rewarding, insightful and invigorating approaches which enhance your business leadership. Moreover, they are techniques for tapping hidden profits and rapid problem solving. They might be the difference between obsolescence and fortune.

The Art of Brainstorming

The term 'Brainstorming' was coined by Alex Osborn, an American advertising executive who introduced the concept in his 1942 book *'How to Think Up'*. His later work, *'Applied Imagination'* published in 1953 brought the term to prominence.

The concept is simple enough: seek solutions to a given problem by capturing the spontaneous output of ideas from one or many individuals. Naturally, one can Brainstorm alone as well as in a group but there's no doubt that groups are best.

You might use these techniques for:

○ Conceiving a company or product name and logo

○ How to reduce costs

○ How to improve any business process

○ Creating an original marketing plan

○ How to reduce wastage in a manufacturing process

○ Working with accountants to devise more efficient financial structure

Indeed, Brainstorming is for almost any topic to which the outcome is required to me more than a simple yes or no. An accountant might brainstorm with the management team about how to raise additional funding, or that team might explore new ways to pay commission to the sales team. Marketers and engineers use the techniques together to design new websites and applications.

The Practise of Brainstorming

Are you a 'morning person'? You may be surprised to discover that mornings are not then your most creative time of day. The opposite may hold true for many of your team.

It's worth experimenting just so you see the results yourself, but a 2012 study analysed 428 students and revealed that "During our optimal time of day we are better at focusing in on a task and eliminating distractions which is beneficial for tasks that require more focused and linear thinking." In short, if we want to be creative and have original thought, then we are more likely to achieve this at our 'worst' time of day.

Mareike Wieth of Albion College and Rose Sacks of Michigan State University who conducted the study posed the question: "Is it diffuse thinking or constrained thinking?" Wieth says, as a good rule of thumb, if it's the former, do it when you're not as fresh, and if it's the latter, pick the time when you're really on. So, morning people, brainstorm in the afternoon.

As the leader, you will need to take time and practise for your team to open up and participate fully. If you're 'the boss', unless you have a really special relationship with your staff they're still going to tend to be reluctant to participate fully at first.

... the participants need to know they can speak up and be heard, and that you will listen ...

It's not a critique of your management style, but in the normal corporate world subordinates are trained to be deferential ... and for brainstorming that's like tying the arms of a juggler: it just doesn't work. Bring your team on board slowly and choose some easier topics: the participants need to know they can speak up and be heard, and that you will listen. Remember, the introverts have ideas too ... now you need to coax them.

Brainstorming doesn't hinge upon the number of participants, but the most is gained when there are at least six people, while more than twelve can become unwieldy. Osborn himself suggested twelve as ideal. It certainly does depend on the topic, but fresh, new, ideas flow at a much faster rate when more people are able they feed off each other's suggestions.

Introducing new skill sets can be most helpful. Sometimes it's the most junior member of the company who has the brightest idea, and I've seen a warehouseman in an IT company propose something which generated massive profits. The adage of not being able to see the wood for all of the trees holds very true for those of us mired in business.

5 Rules for Successful Brainstorming

You've assembled your group, you've given a little brief on the objective, and you've asked everyone to join in. So now you need everyone to understand that Brainstorming is a process: it's not enough to just write down ideas. That's not to say you won't benefit, but the real rewards come the first time you approach the problem with tried-and-true methodologies. I believe these five rules which follow should be printed and handed to all attendees, that is how critical they are to achieve real success:

#1 QUANTITY VS. QUALITY

To be effective, the participants must write everything which comes to mind, without critiquing or 'picking the thought apart' at the outset. To do otherwise is to shut down that person's willingness to contribute.

2 CRITICISE LATER

The surest damper to successful brainstorming is for the group leader or other participants to scorn any suggestion. No negative comments, please! There must be a free flow of ideas, and the environment is best if job titles are checked at the door: the warehouse clerk might offer the key thought overlooked by the computer programmer.

3 WELCOME THE WILD SIDE

Suspend assumptions. Almost no idea - or thought - is too radical to be included. Even something offered in jest can trigger a thought process from which further ideas might flow. As the adjudicator, you need to ensure everyone is heard. Oh, and laughter helps the ideas flow.

4 RECORD, COMBINE AND IMPROVE

As the ideas flow there will be threads which start to crystallise, and from there it will be apparent that more emphasis might be warranted in certain directions. Combine these thoughts and create new core areas upon which to focus. Expand the thought processes, never contract.

5 ENGAGE ENOUGH PEOPLE

Brainstorming doesn't hinge upon the number of participants, but the most is gained when there are between six and 12 people. More can work, and I've participated in extraordinary sessions of 40 participants. Osborn himself suggested 12 as ideal.

The Next Step: Mind Map

The term Mind Map, incidentally, was coined by an Englishman named Tony Buzan who introduced the term 'mind map' during a 1974 BBC TV series he hosted, called *'Use Your Head'*.

The development of the technique started with 'Fish Bones', became freer with 'Spider Diagrams' and morphed into the computer-generated process which today we call Mind Maps. That said, there's nothing about the process which requires a computer.

The premise is simple: you start with a thought in the centre and then lines radiate from that point in all directions … figuratively looking like a child's drawing of a spider from above. This approach shrugs off structures and encourages the flow of ideas.

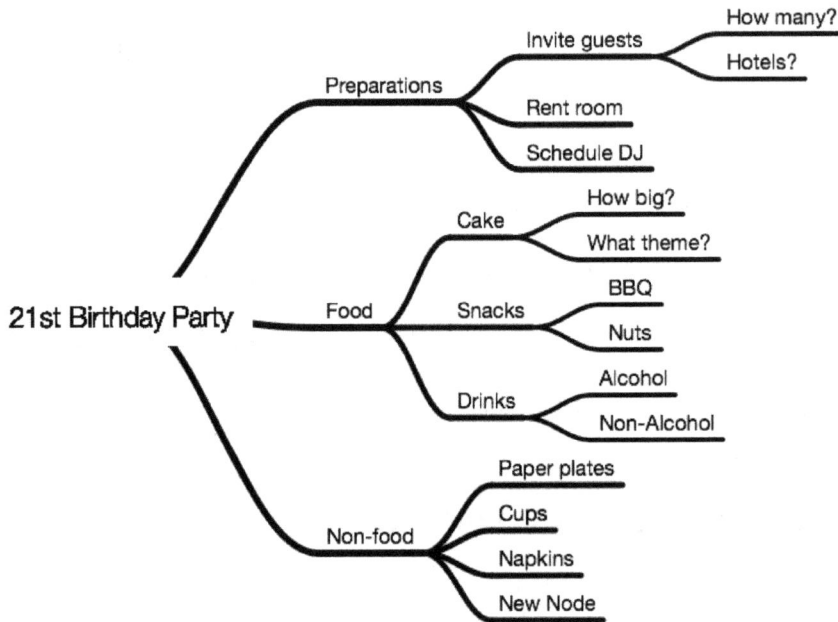

Whether called brainstorming, visual thinking or mind mapping, the concept remains the same: to set one's thoughts out in a graphical, non-linear form.

A simple Mind Map might look like the example above after just a few moments. Notice how ideas and tasks can branch off of each other, and how the pattern encourages free thinking as opposed to making a linear list.

Remember, the key is to let the ideas and thoughts flow and not to be distracted by software options or even spelling. Hundreds, even thousands, of nodes are supported, and each may be 'collapsed' individually to avoid distraction, or linked to form connected sub-topics, as in the example below.

With some software packages you can embed all manner of media, including photographs, handwriting, audio and video.

TONY BUZAN'S 7 STEPS TO MAKING A MIND MAP

With more than forty years of thought and development of the concept, Tony Buzan is surely the authority on Mind Maps. In practise, his opinions bear fruit and his guiding principles are paraphrased here:

1. Start in the centre of a blank page turned sideways (landscape) because starting in the centre gives your brain freedom to express itself more freely and naturally.

2. Use an image for your central idea because an image prompts you use your imagination. A central image is more interesting, helps you concentrate, and gives your brain more of a buzz!

3. Use colours throughout because colours are as exciting to your brain as are images. Colour adds tremendous energy to your creative thinking.

4. Connect your main branches to the central image and connect other branches from there because your brain works by association. It likes to link things together.

5. Make your branches curved rather than straight-lined because having nothing but straight lines is boring to your brain and stifles imagination.

6. Use one key word per line because single key words give your mind map more power and flexibility.

7. Use images throughout because each image, like the central image, is also worth a thousand words.

Choosing Software for Mind Mapping

There are free packages for both Windows and Apple operating systems, but there's much to be gained from paying the money for a proven and better supported application.

FOR THE APPLE MAC OPERATING SYSTEM

MindNode (www.mindnode.com) free, but you'll probably want the full version for $19.99 through the Apple Store. Truly intuitive, this is excellent for the beginner and has the advantage of enabling the user to get on with the task rather than risk getting bogged down with options.

iMindMap (www.imindmap.com) free, or £7.50 per month. Created in collaboration with Tony Buzan this has almost every option one could seek, offering as it does Buzan's concepts of combining colour, fluidity and media.

CLOUD BASED

Coggle (www.coggle.it) is a 'must see', not least of all because it's priced at $5.00 per month and it's simple to use: you just sign into it with your google account and off you go. There's nothing to install as it's web based. There are extensive features which enable you to add colour and to reposition your thoughts, and the finished results export as very useful PDF files or PNG images.

There are many other Mind Mapping applications but these represent the best-of-the-best. Of course, no software is actually needed since a flip chart page and a marker pen achieve the same result, but you will be surprised at how quickly a single page can fill.

Unleash your Creativity

The most innovative business leaders encourage Mind Maps to become routine parts of departmental business. The very process is so involving that it not only adds to employee satisfaction but it nurtures a philosophy that every employee counts. Used wisely, and manufacturers see their quality improve, software developers see their applications require fewer fixes, and sales departments see more sales successes. The list is endless.

The Benefit of Early SWOT Analysis

The one part of a business plan unfamiliar to many people is the S.W.O.T. Analysis. It's not complicated, but every financier expects to see it included.

The principle is easy: you chart the four components upon which your business is based:

O Strengths

O Weaknesses

O Opportunities

O Threats

A well-established management concept, it was conceived in the early 1960's by Albert Humphrey of Stanford University in the USA. His research was into the success and failure of corporate planning, and the four categories identified gave rise to S.O.F.T. Analysis.

> _"What is good in the present is Satisfactory, good in the future is an Opportunity; bad in the present is a Fault and bad in the future is a Threat."_

In 1964, 'Fault' was replaced by 'Weakness' and S.W.O.T. was established. It's a valuable tool across the management spectrum and is used today in a variety of disciplines.

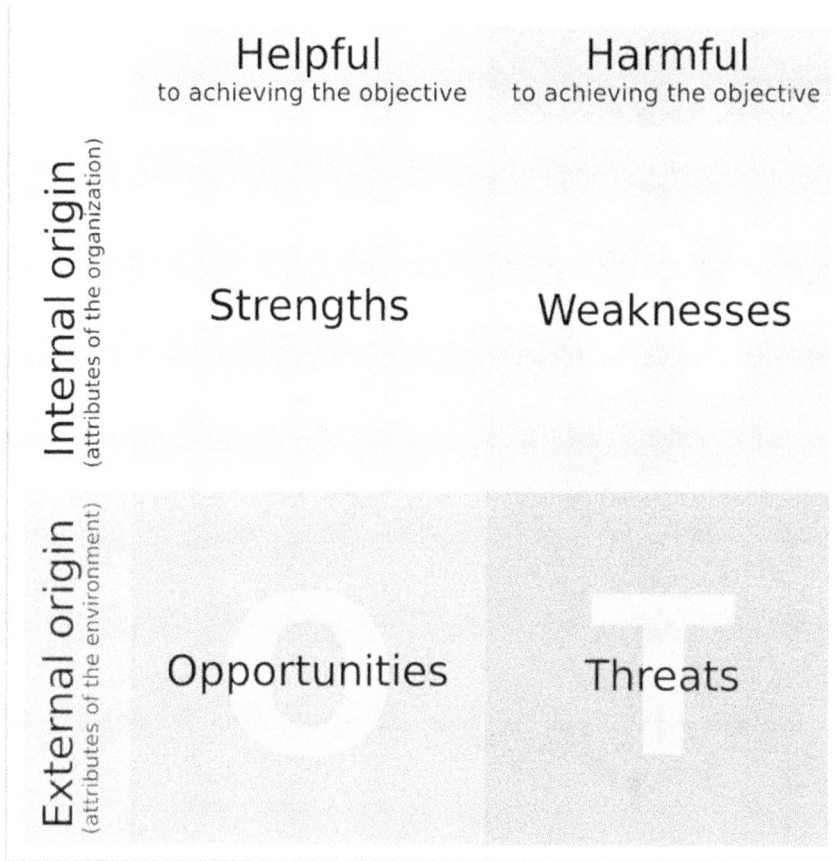

Use S.W.O.T in the Early Stages

Before you invest too much time in your idea, create a S.W.O.T. analysis to reveal the shortcomings and consider how they might be overcome. This technique can separate the hair-brained thought processes from the real gems, and encourage lateral thinking from which a solid business plan may be created.

STRENGTHS

These are the tangible and intangible attributes of your business. They may relate to your people or your product. Above all, they are internal and within the ability of your organisation to control.

WEAKNESSES

Factors about your business which are threats to the business goals and objectives. What might be improved to diminish these weaknesses.

OPPORTUNITIES

Positive external factors which represent the reason for the business to be created, especially commercial market gaps. May include business, environment, people, places and timing

THREATS

These are strictly external factors over which the organisation has no control. Examples might include broad or macro-economic factors, a competitor replicating your product, or indeed any factor which could harm your business and interfere with the achievement of your goals.

Example S.W.O.T. Analysis

Strengths

- Management have industry experience and strong reputation
- Extensive client contacts
- Lowest production cost per unit
- Product is innovative
- Lowest infrastructure costs
- Our product is a 'must have' for business, not a 'nice to have'
- Many ideas for product diversification

Weaknesses

- Market newcomer – must start with client base of zero
- Identified with our past employers
- High cost of staff with required skills
- Less funding than the competition
- Marketplace still immature and technology could change

Opportunities

- No other vendor offering similar services
- Marketplace seeking better customer support
- Exceptional market demand and not enough suppliers
- Drop shipping from manufacturer will reduce freight costs
- Competition not using e-Commerce

Threats

- Service offering relatively easy to replicate
- Competition launching marketing campaign with exceptional funding
- Competitors deliver quality products
- Exchange rates could turn adverse
- Fuel costs could impact delivery and margins

General Considerations

- *Naming your Business*
- *Company Formation*
- *The Shareholders Agreement*
- *Advantages of Business Incubators*
- *Non-Executive Directors*

<u>Naming your Business</u>

There exists a company with the name of '*Alhaj Raqub Plastic Packaging Complex Company Limited*'. In the digital age, this is obviously not an approach which will help either them or their customers.

The company name was not always as complex a process as it is today but, as the economy has become global through the emergence of the internet, there are many considerations, the first of which is to understand that you must not impinge upon the trademark of another product or business entity.

Your investment in name, brand, logos, marketing, web domains, customer relations, email databases and more can be undone in an instant when challenged by lawyers' letters from a multi-national corporation. They are increasingly aggressive and no business of any size is immune. To make this mistake can be devastating.

For example, in 2015 the famous Everton Football Club initiated legal proceedings against Everton Farm Shop located in the Nottinghamshire village of Everton. Despite the town name dated back to the Middle Ages (it means *Wild Boar*), and despite the fact that the farm shop is run by a family of farmers raising organic pigs in that village, the proprietor is being forced to change the name, logo and other materials.

UK Law

There is ample reference material online at the government site www.gov.uk which will guide you, but essential considerations include the following:

○ Avoid 'too like' names such as 'Dynamic Technology LLP' which is too like 'Dinamix Technology LLP';

○ Avoid 'same as' names, for example: 'Hands UK Ltd' and 'Hand's Ltd' are the same as 'Hands Ltd', and 'Box.com Ltd' is too similar to 'Box Ltd'. Adding punctuation does not make one name sufficiently different;

○ Avoid so-called 'sensitive words' within the name, such as 'assurance', 'fund', and other words which imply a registered financial institution;

You may also use the free Companies House service for checking potential conflicts. Your searches will result is alerts when your idea is too close to an already registered name.

Your quest doesn't stop there, though, as searching for a company name doesn't mean that your concept isn't being used by a charity, as a trademark or in some other fashion and is thus protected.

General Considerations

In the UK there are 2 million businesses, 2.3 million limited companies, 2.5 million trademarks, 7 million European trademarks, and 4 million domain names - that is over 10 million UK trading names, and yet you must register your business name even if you are a sole trader!

○ The name must lend itself to use on the internet, not least of all it must be resilient to misspellings. As a 'digital age' founder, you will want to avoid words which cause spelling confusion between British English and US English, such as *'Colour vs. Color'*, and *'Honour vs. Honor'*, to offer but two examples;

○ How will it look when printed on business literature? Names which begin with the letters I and L can become difficult, such as 'Iliad';

○ Does the name have an unexpected connotation in overseas markets? Think here of the American Chevrolet car called the *'Nova'* which, too late, was mocked for being the Spanish of *'No Go'*. There are countless other examples!

○ Brevity is paramount, not least of all for the ease of creating a domain name but also for linking with whichever logo you adopt;

Suggestions

Don't worry if you can't come up with something immediately. Experiment with combinations such as combining a colour, shape, animal, letter or object to form the name. Proven successful examples include:

○ Blue Circle (as in Blue Circle Industries);

○ Square D (as in Square D Company Inc.);

○ Red Hat (as in Red Hat Technologies);

○ … and many others!

Give thought as to whether you want a location-based name such as 'London IT Experts', which will certainly do well for pitching your products within London, and will generate more traffic from google searches, but is it not restricting your geographic reach?

Abstract names such as 'The Pink Elephant', tell nothing about you but open huge possibilities for creative marketing. Even more abstract are words you invent, often by adding a prefix or suffix to a word. An excellent example is that of the British charity, AFRICALITY. They took a root word, Africa, and added the suffix. It has no true meaning and yet in ten letters created something unique and entirely relevant to their objective in a crowded market.

There's also the possibility of creating a prestigious sounding name out of the blue by using surname combinations, but do your due diligence with great care to avoid nasty letters from lawyers a year later.

Finally, don't overlook the use of foreign words or names, especially those from the Latin, Greek, Spanish and Italian languages. These are often ripe for creating root words, but please research their true meaning.

Names and the Internet

Notwithstanding the legal complexities, you must be found by your target audience and since you are in the Digital Age your marketing will be paramount. Given that you might also have your website and collateral translated into multiple languages, consider these pointers for your company name:

○ Is it memorable? It should go without saying, so why do so many businesses have such tedious names?

○ Is it easy to spell? So *'Euro Express IT'* would become *'euroexpressit'* which is easy enough, but do avoid odd spellings such as *'xpress'*.

○ Make it work without hyphens, underscores, periods or special characters. The one exception to this rule is the strudel or '@' symbol.

○ Avoid potentially confusing letter combinations. Consider the name *'Illiana'* and how awkward it is to read in a sans serif font like this.

○ If your business relies on marketing to a particular location then incorporate a place, region, or country name. If you offer a particular focussed product or service, then by all means incorporate it too. For example, 'Midlands Marketing', 'Scotland Printers', 'London Law' are immediately descriptive and help boost your rankings in search engines.

Make a Mind Map

Here's where you can really make use of a Mind Map! Start with your industry in the centre and create branches from there. To get you started, it might look something like in the example below.

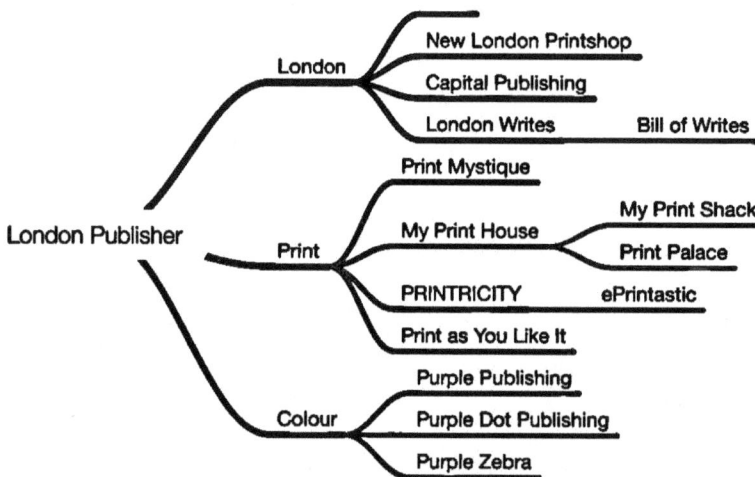

```
                                    New London Printshop
                        London
                                    Capital Publishing

                                    London Writes        Bill of Writes

                              Print Mystique
                                                         My Print Shack
                                    My Print House
London Publisher        Print                            Print Palace

                                    PRINTRICITY          ePrintastic

                              Print as You Like It

                                    Purple Publishing
                        Colour      Purple Dot Publishing
                                    Purple Zebra
```

Don't be reluctant, and gather friends and family around. A child is as likely to offer a valid suggestion as you, sometimes more so. It's a fun process!

Company Formation

Choosing the appropriate business structure is a relatively simple process, not least of all because one can change the legal formation at any later date: if you start with a partnership you can reform it as a limited company.

The four legal structures you will be considering in the United Kingdom are:

1. Sole Trader
2. Ordinary Business Partnership
3. Limited Partnership and Limited Liability Partnership
4. Limited Company

At the outset it is important to note that if your venture will qualify for the HMRC SEIS scheme, with all of the associated tax advantages for you and potential investors, then only a Limited Company will suffice.

Sole Trader

You may opt to start as a sole trader, in other words you are working for yourself and you are classed as self-employed. There is no requirement to register with HMRC.

You can employ staff. 'Sole trader' means you're responsible for the business, not that you have to work alone.

The key advantages are the sheer simplicity and absence of any up-front costs. The money you make is yours to keep, minus your obligation to report profits on your tax return and to pay income tax.

The key disadvantage is that you take personal liability for any losses your business makes. If your business accumulates debts and must be closed, then your creditors can seize your assets.

Ordinary Business Partnership

An Ordinary Business Partnership is a legal entity with a registered business name. This is the simplest structure to use if entering business with one or more other people.

You and your partners hold personal liability for all debts and, effectively, the obligations and risks are the same as being a sole trader.

Note that in Scotland a 'partnership' is referred to as a firm and carries its own legal identity.

From a tax perspective, all partners must submit a personal 'Self-Assessment' tax return annually.

Limited Partnership and Limited Liability Partnership

Insulating oneself from the risk of business failure and the resultant debts, or claims for damages against the business prompts many partnerships to select one of two improved legal structures: the Limited Partnership or the Limited Liability Partnership

The liability for debts that can't be paid in a Limited Partnership is split among partners. 'General Partners' run the business and can be personally liable, whereas 'Limited Partners' carry liability equal to their investment.

In a Limited Liability Partnership (LLP), the partners' liability is restricted to the amount of money they invested in the business.

From a tax perspective the obligations are the same as for an Ordinary Business Partnership.

Limited Company

A limited company is an organisation which runs your business. It is a separate legal entity, and its finances are separate to your personal finances.

The profits generated are owned by the company itself, not by you. Once it pays the required corporation tax, the profit may be shared among the shareholders.

Ownership is defined by those who hold the shares in the company (referred to as 'members'). The members may, or may not, be directors.

Most limited companies are 'limited by shares'. This means that the shareholders' responsibilities for the company's financial liabilities are limited to the value of shares that they own but haven't paid for. This might mean the members have a total liability of as little as £50 each.

The alternative limited company structure is where the directors or shareholders establish a company limited by guarantee. In this case, their total financial risk is equal only to the value of that guarantee.

The key advantage of a limited company is that it protects the shareholders from personal liability for debts, with the proviso that no debts were accumulated illegally.

Credit with suppliers is easier to establish with a limited company, and all the more so if the share capital issued is substantially above the minimum required. For example, a limited company established with £6,000 of share capital can often secure credit within weeks of opening. Your suppliers can see that there is some assurance that they can realise payment if you default.

The tax advantages are numerous: the limited company must pay corporation tax, but this is at a rate well below income tax levels, and there are numerous approaches one may utilise to reduce the income tax burden on the shareholders.

The key obligations upon the company are that it must complete statutory accounts, submit an annual return to Companies House, and file a company tax return with HMRC.

Taxation Considerations

In the event that your business doesn't qualify for SEIS investment, an LLP partnership offers various tax advantages.

Members of an LLP are liable to income tax and National Insurance Contributions (NIC) with respect to the profits, however these are less than the equivalent payable for employees.

It is less tax-efficient for shareholders or directors of a limited company to receive a regular salary, than to receive a profit allocation from an LLP due to the difference in NIC levels. The upshot is that if the bulk of the profits will be distributed each year, then the LLP is the more tax-efficient legal structure.

However, if the business retains profits for re-investment back into the business, then a company could be more tax-efficient because the rate of corporation tax in the UK is very low compared with other jurisdictions.

Finally, it should be noted that an LLP can add and remove members with considerable ease. This is in contrast to the Limited Company, for which the formalities are often quite considerable.

An accountant will review your anticipated profits and objectives and will be able to advise on the most efficient legal structure from a taxation perspective.

The Shareholders Agreement

While the legal entity of the company itself is governed by the Articles of Association, it is the Shareholders' Agreement (SHA) which defines exactly how the company shall be run and how disputes shall be handled. Think of it as a pre-nuptial agreement for companies.

The Articles of Association define the constitution of the company, and is a contract between the shareholders and the company. It is held at Company's House and remains a public document.

The Shareholders Agreement, however, is a private document and it regulates the relationship between the shareholders and governs how they shall perform their duties, run the company, and manage disputes.

No document is more critical to your financial security. Even lifelong friends and family members fall out, and with large sums of money involved the potential for a simple misunderstanding to erupt is ever-present: the press is full of tales of such disputes.

This legal document covers the following essential topics:

O The rights and obligations of shareholders;

O The rules regarding the sale or transfer of shares;

O The process by which new shares may be issued;

O The day to day management of the company;

O How shall management decisions be made;

O Financial governance (loans, dividends);

O The sale or dissolution of the company;

O The resolution of disputes between shareholders;

The Shareholders' Agreement should be constructed at the time the company is registered and before the investment has begun. Even between friends, this creates a professional mind-set and in no way is insulting to propose.

The Specifics

A key aspect of the Shareholder's Agreement is that it affords protection to minority shareholders. It avoids the majority shareholders from using their combined shares to the detriment of those in the minority.

Under UK company law, majority shareholders have considerable power: they can issue new shares which dilute the shareholding of current owners, they can appoint new Directors – such as friends or family – and the minority have no legal basis on which to object.

The SHA can stipulate which types of decision require unanimous agreement or, perhaps, stipulate that certain decisions require the approval of a specific shareholder, and the examples above are typical.

Day to day management decisions which are often included can detail a full list of obligations. These might cover financial matters, such as loans, mortgages and overdraft arrangements, the approved levels of borrowing, and the payment of salaries and dividends.

Do you Need a Solicitor?

While the services of a solicitor are highly recommended, this must be balanced by the costs: a Shareholders' Agreement can be a complex document.

Fees for contracting the professional services for drafting this highly customised document vary wildly, with quotations ranging from £500 to in excess of £10,000. For the primary investors, it will be some of the wisest money ever spent.

While a solicitor is best, there are many sample Shareholders' Agreement templates online, one of the best of which was created by a collection of prestigious law firms on behalf of the UK Business Angels Association. This organisation offers their superb PDF template online free of charge to their members.

By all means use this template – your solicitor will thank you – but do make a commitment to have it fully tailored within a reasonable time-frame, such as when filing your first set of accounts.

Non-executive Directors

Non-executive Directors (NED) are an important yet often overlooked function within the SME sector, and most particularly in respect to start-ups. More than a mentor, the NED undertakes many of the obligations as any other director, but in an entirely different capacity.

> *"The Non-Executive Director should bring an independent judgment to bear on issues of strategy, performance and resources including key appointments and standards of conduct." – The Cadbury Report*

Their focus is upon board matters, not on the day to day administration and decision making. They bring to the business special knowledge, experience, objectivity and a 'guiding hand' to assist the directors. They are, effectively, 'private counsel', to be consulted as required.

Duties & Responsibilities

Directors rely on the non-executive for matters such as creating or refining the strategic direction of the business, expecting the response to be creative, informative and constructive. Objectivity is important.

Performance monitoring is part of the role, and any new business benefits from a trusted outsider, deeply familiar with the business plan, to evaluate operations. For example, if revenues fall consistently below expectation, the NED will work with the directors to establish why, perhaps delivering some blunt assessments.

The NED has a legal duty to review the financial reports of the company to the extent that they are satisfied with their integrity. They will advise if they perceive risks, and propose strategies for the reduction of risks.

As a spokesperson for the business the NED also has a role: the company might rely on the NED to represent them in certain situations, such as with the media, or to interface with solicitors in the event of legal dispute.

Why your Business Needs a NED

Apart from fulfilling their legal duties, the Non-executive Director fulfils the role of trusted advisor and mediator to the directors. Frequently, lenders or external investors will want a non-executive director on the board to bring an external perspective to represent their interests. This is especially true with respect to the expansion of a family company. There is no doubt that your appeal to any lender is greatly enhanced by the presence and foresight in making such an appointment.

> *… the executive directors use the NED as a resource for diffusing internal conflict …*

In their advisory capacity, such matters of whether or not to seek further financing can be complex for those too closely involved. Alternatively, are there obvious business deficiencies which are being ignored by the directors for any variety of reasons? The Non-executive becomes both a 'sounding board' and a teacher.

The value of the Non-executive to the small business is inestimable when the pressures of growing a business start to take their toll. The Shareholders' Agreement is only to be reverted to as a last resort, and by then it may be too late. By bringing a Non-executive director on board at the very earliest stages, the executive directors use the NED as a resource for diffusing internal conflict which, all too often, is the root of failure for the small business.

Remuneration

There is no standard remuneration, but as very much a part-time role, the Non-executive might be compensated with a fixed monthly allowance. This might be supplemented further with a specified number of shares, an established dividend or some combination of the above.

Make no underestimation of the legal responsibility of the role, and think of appropriate compensation.

Given the advantage the non-executive should bring to the business, it is reasonable to propose that the company shall provide Directors Liability Insurance.

Choosing your NED

Recruitment tends to be via informal business networks, which for the SME might include making approaches to senior business figures well known to the directors.

Consider which business people you know well and admire? Perhaps you know a Managing Director who is in the long progress of making a hand-over to their successor? It might be a respected businessman heading for retirement and appreciative of the opportunity to keep themselves occupied by doing what they know best?

Recruitment agencies are also an option, but the costs often outweigh the advantages. Placing an advertisement in a relevant trade or professional publications is more cost effective and leads to better results.

Interviews, background checks and unanimous agreement of the directors are mandatory. Your goal is to establishing that your team can work with the non-executive in terms of personality, approach, and management style.

Financing Options

- *The Magic of SEIS*
- *Sources of Funding*
- *Raising your Start-up Stake*

The Magic of SEIS

Can you imagine a scheme in which an investor might make a £50,000 investment into your business but have their potential loss limited to just £13,750. Too good to be true? It exists: it's called the Seed Enterprise Investment Scheme, SEIS for short, and it's run by the HMRC.

> *It is summarised as offering remarkable tax relief and absolute protection of capital gains.*

The scheme was introduced in 2011, and it represents a revolution in delivering tax incentives for investors. It is summarised as offering remarkable tax relief and absolute protection of capital gains. Here's an example of how it works:

> *Jack is a higher rate tax payer and he invests £50,000 in ABC Ltd. At the outset, he receives £15,000 of tax relief on his initial investment. This is paid through a tax rebate. After five years he sells his shares for £5,000, giving him a loss of £30,000. Jack now gets income tax relief of 45%, which is £13,500. The investor has just limited his net loss to £16,500 rather than £45,000.'*

Assuming the business makes a profit, the capital gains are waived and the tax relief already secured is 'money in the pocket'. What of the success story? Here is the other outcome:

'After five years or more, Jack sells his shares in ABC Ltd. for £300,000. Jack invested £50,000 and gained £15,000 of tax relief. His total profit is £265,000 … all of which is tax free.'

Business Angels and Venture Capitalists know about SEIS, and the similar EIS scheme. Examining your business plan to see if you qualify is an imperative, and it might make you re-invent your business plan altogether. With all other parameters broadly the same, few investors would select a non-SEIS qualifying business over one which qualifies. The scheme is generous in the extreme, but this is commensurate with the high-risk nature of investing in start-ups.

Conditions on the Investor

The shares must be held for a period of 3 years, from date of issue, for relief to be retained. If they are disposed of within that 3-year period, or if any of the qualifying conditions cease to be met during that period, relief will be withdrawn or reduced.

Relief is available at 50% of the cost of the shares, on a maximum annual investment of £100,000. The relief is given by way of a reduction of tax liability, providing there is sufficient tax liability against which to set it. A claim to relief can be made up to 5 years after the 31 January following the tax year in which the investment was made.

Conditions on the Company

The SEIS scheme is not complex and does not require specialist advice, although the services of an accountant are to be welcomed. The key features of the company include certain specifics. Specifically, the company must:

- Not have fewer than 25 employees, and if it is a parent company, then the figure applies to the whole group;
- Not have no more than £200,000 in gross assets;
- Not have had investment from a Venture Capital Trust;
- Not receive more than £150,000 via the total of the SEIS scheme or other government aid;
- Be less than two years old, and consist of new trade;
- Not be controlled by another company;

○ Must exist solely for the purpose of carrying on a qualifying trade.

None of the above are particularly onerous, and there is no limit as to the total potential investment: the restriction is only upon that part which qualifies for the special tax reliefs.

Business Activities and 'Qualifying Trades'

HMRC define a qualifying trade as 'one which is conducted on a commercial basis with a view to the realisation of profit'. For the purposes of SEIS, most trades qualify but some are excluded. The SEIS business must not consist of more than 20% of an excluded trade or activity.

Here is a summary of the most popular activities which are excluded:

○ Almost any financial activity including the letting of assets.

○ Trade in goods, other than retail or wholesale.

○ Receiving royalties or licence fees except as a result of intangible assets created by the company itself.

○ Legal or accountancy services.

○ Land or property development, including farming, market gardening or almost any forestry activity.

○ Operating or managing hotels or comparable establishments such as nursing or residential care homes.

Summary

There is no more attractive proposition to an investor with UK tax liabilities than the SEIS and the EIS schemes. It delivers massive downside risk containment, and on the upside it offers the absolute realisation of total protection of all capital gains.

Formally registering your company and securing HMRC SEIS approval in advance of going to market for investment is highly recommended. As to your business plan itself, your SEIS or EIS qualification is should be emphasised strongly.

Sources of Funding

While Business Angels and Venture Capitalists are nothing new, access to them is easier than ever before. Each have their niche, benefits and pitfalls. Of particular interest is the intermediate approach called Crowd Funding.

Business Angels

Business Angels, also known as Angel Investors, are generally High Net Worth individuals seeking above average returns on a portion of their capital.

There are many thousands world-wide, and numerous networks online through which one may be connected. Very often, they work in syndicates, so spreading the risk when investing in a start-up.

Business Angels tend to seek investments which range between £10,000 and £500,000 and in return they seek part-ownership of your company. This alone is a factor for you to consider: is there any way for you to kick start your business without giving up some part at the outset?

Advantages of Business Angel financing include:

O Ideal for high risk investments such as start-ups;

O Rapid decision making process;

O Have a vested interest in your success and will leverage their own contacts.

O Often a wealth of business experience, typically within your industry, upon which you may draw.

O No demand for collateral or security, interest or other repayment.

As noted above, with a Business Angel you are, in effect, selling part of your company at the outset. This may have considerable benefits to the founders in terms of reduction of risk of their own capital, but the cost of that 'loan' can be regretted when the business starts to realise substantial returns or is being sold for a tidy profit.

As a rule of thumb, Business Angels are seeking an ROI based upon their investment multiplied by the number of years: for example, if the investment is £25,000 for five years, then the anticipated return on their capital should be £250,000.

Venture Capitalists

Venture capital funding is a more advanced form of funding than offered by the Business Angel. It's a form of private equity investment providing unsecured funding in exchange for a share of the equity in the business.

Venture Capitalists, or VC's as they are often known, are businesses which are funded by major financial institutions, such as insurance or pension funds. They have one goal: to drive the aggressive growth of their investment in order that in five years they may float the enterprise on the stock exchange and realise huge returns.

Approximately only 20% of VC investments are made into seed or start-up ventures. The VC's in this field tend to be specialists, and they are certainly not the norm.

VC's seek opportunities to invest £500,000 to £5m, and they are most attracted to businesses which have proven their products and filed several years of accounts.

Advantages of VC Funding include:

O Access to very large cash investments;

O A pool of significant management expertise;

O Success can deliver massive financial rewards;

O Often, but not always, advantageous 'door opening' for access to new markets;

Disadvantages of VC Funding Include:

O Onerous reporting obligations;

O Extreme control of the business;

O Conflicting cultural approaches and methods;

O Demands for an extremely large or even a controlling shareholding;

O One or more VC members sitting on your board;

Access to Venture Capitalists is complex, and it is most frequently facilitated through senior levels at one's bank or a large firm of accountants. Be warned that only a very small percentage of proposals are accepted.

If your business has exceptional growth, and the board have both a true vision and the experience to match, then a VC might be suitable. As a rule of thumb, though, remember that this route is most typically valid for businesses with a turnover of > £5m.

Your entire business structure will have to be impeccable, and your internal financial controls stringent and expert at every level. The process is gruelling, and can involve considerable travel, expense. Win or lose, you will emerge on the other side as a vastly more experienced business person.

Crowd Funding

Crowd Funding has appeared as a revolutionary means of raising funding, delivering results for the very smallest of start-ups to companies with considerable expertise and backing.

Depending upon the project, it may be possible for an investor to stump up just £5 for a 'piece of the action'. Indeed, many people are spreading the risk by putting £100 on each of twenty or more projects. Some will fail, just as others will succeed. So let's explore what's on offer and what might be a good fit for your business.

BUSINESS LOANS

At its simplest, crowd funding represents access to straight-forward loans. One of the more established firms, such as <u>Funding Circle</u>, offer a peer-to-peer platform for investment in the form of loans to UK based SME's. To date they have raised loans of £1.2 billion from more than 48,000 people to 15,000 businesses. The average return on investment is 7.3%. If you're already in business, then this is an excellent approach for a business seeking to raise some cash, but it's not of much use to a start-up.

INVOICE FACTORING

There's a new form of peer-to-peer lending as typified by <u>Market Invoice Limited</u>. Their approach is to enable a business to sell their invoices online and generate immediate cash flow. The costs vary, but 1-3% of the face value of the invoice is the norm.

This firm alone has funded almost £700m invoices so far, and continues to grow.

If invoice factoring is required for your business, then this is an excellent approach to reduce the costs when compared to normal business to business service vendors.

START-UP FUNDING

The UK market for online crowd funding remains rather niche when compared to the United States. An example is <u>Crowd Funder</u>, which attracts a modest number of start-up businesses and which offers a platform to secure investment within thirty or sixty days.

Businesses usually offer something tangible in return for the investment, a product or service to be delivered following the launch. Examples include those planning to open restaurants who offer some number of free meals proportionate to the sum invested.

The <u>Crowd Cube</u> platform is at the top level, offering equity investments to registered UK Limited companies. Start-ups are welcome, but be prepared to submit detailed financial forecasts, a full business plan, and time to develop a sophisticated 'pitch'. Note that they highlight the imperative of having received SEIS approval from HMRC, mentioning that without such approval funding is highly unlikely.

Their success includes having raised £152m for 384 projects, drawing on investments from more than 270,000 registered investors.

The Crowd Cube projects vary considerably, spanning energy, food, high-tech, software development and more. The businesses seeking funding are large and small, with some seeking only £20,000 and others £2m.

Summary

Crowdfunding is here to stay, and with improved regulation will get stronger still. Approaching high street banks and Business Angels is a process which can take anywhere up to twelve months, whereas a crowd funding exercise will conclude in 30-60 days.

It's an approach which doesn't suit everyone, but the affordability of the financing is beyond reproach, as is the flexibility.

Raising your Start-up Stake

Armed with your business plan, going to the High Street Bank for a business loan might not be quite the worst decision you ever made, but it's not going to win you any prizes. Every penny of debt must be serviced, and despite interest rates being at record lows, the banks are still charging double-digit rates.

That £25,000 loan at 12.5% is for 60 months will cost you monthly repayments of £562, and in the bargain you will have paid £8,747 in interest. At 16% the same loan will see you paying £11,477 in interest! As a start-up, the rule of thumb is to try to avoid the banks if at all possible.

Suppose you have £10,000 and need £80,000 to launch your business, with satisfactory room to cover your cash flow. How might you approach the challenge?

Step 1: Release your Assets!

If you're a home owner, then you might have accumulated equity in your flat or home. Perhaps that could be accessed? Similarly, if you're over fifty-five years of age, you might qualify to release some portion of your pension.

If employed, then cut back on all expenditures for a few months. Downsize the car, cancel the premium cable television package, stop eating out and trim back on the luxuries. You won't have time for them anyhow. It adds up quickly.

If you're serious about the venture, you have to prove it. Approach your family and friends too for a secured personal loan guaranteed an asset? For the sake of argument, let's assume you've now secured £20,000 of cash. It's reasonable.

Step 2: Partnership

You've written a good business plan, so would the business generate enough cash to support a second partner? The advantages of a business partner are considerable.

With your £20,000 of cash, you might propose a matching investment from the incoming partner, form a limited company and together you move forward. That's £40,000 found, £40,000 more required.

Step 3: SEIS

You and your partner register the limited company with HMRC and gain SEIS approval. Now you gain each gain tax relief for the preceding year and the current year combined. Let's suppose this nets the two of you a total rebate of £15,000. You now have £55,000 and you still need another £25,000.

Step 4: Crowd Funding

You can show a product, or at least a solid product concept, you've raised £55,000 and you make a pitch as to why people should consider investing that £25,000.

It's an uncertain world, with many variables, but if your idea has broad appeal it's possible you might make it. However, for the sake of this exercise, you target £10,000 for your fund-raiser as that's more achievable.

By the end of sixty days the push closes and you have pledges of £8,000 – and with 80% of your crowd-funding goal you did well. You've now got £63,000, still £17,000 shy of your start-up demand.

Step 5: Friends and Family

Now you have a business plan, a product, cash, and some rather market research: other people believe in your idea and they've parted with their money.

So now ask friends and family for a cash loan at fair interest rates, say 5% or so? They're going to get the SEIS tax rebate too! Or you could offer shares in the company. If you want one person to invest £8,000 – that's 10% of your start-up – and it's entirely unsecured, why not? However, because of the SEIS advantage, they might feel 5% of the business is fair enough. Remember too, their loan is interest free!

Step 6: The Business Angel

Large and small, Business Angels abound. They've not the cheapest route to money but now you only require £9,000 and you've ticked every necessary box to get some immediate interest. Expect a quick decision if you plan is good enough. They will probably want 10% or more of your shares though, even with the SEIS scheme.

Step 7: Back to the Bank

Alternatively, you could now return to the bank and take a £9,000 loan. With all of the evidence you've established you should get a better interest rate, let's say 10.0%. Over 36 months this will cost you just £290 per month with a total interest payable of £1,455.

That is a lot of savings, and you still have control of your business.

Creating the Cost Efficient Business

- *The Business Incubator Advantage*
- *Reducing Office Overheads*
- *People as a Service*
- *Leveraging Technology*
- *Maximising Service Revenue*
- *Subscription Services*

The Business Incubator Advantage

One of the surest ways to improve your chances of success is to kick-start your project under the auspices of a Business Incubator or Accelerator program.

Most commonly, such programs are orientated to businesses involved in 'high technology', although this is not always the case. Success rates for SME's increase to as much as 92%.

Apart from offering guidance across a myriad of topics, the best of such schemes facilitate introductions to customers, financiers and specialist expertise perhaps far beyond your own.

Basing your fledgling business in London, Birmingham and Edinburgh increases your access to such schemes dramatically. Many are run by public sector agencies while others are private enterprises, such as those offered by John Lewis, Telefonica and Barclays Bank.

The lead body for the oversight is UK Business Incubation (UKBI), and it is recognised as such by UK Government. There are more than 300 business incubators in the UK supporting around 12,000 businesses, guiding early-stage businesses on the road to commercial success.

A leading figure in the UK field is Mark Hales, described as a 'serial entrepreneur' and the man behind the money and vision for the creation of the <u>Oxygen Accelerator</u> in Birmingham. Mark said:

> *"I think there's a great need for business accelerators. When I took over a small business back in 1999, the best advice I could get was from the Business Link guy, who'd never run a business in his life and wasn't able to offer that much help. Any environment where you can bring a group of talented, experienced entrepreneurs together is a good thing."*

Whether publicly funded or private, there is opportunity to tap into vast expertise. The programs are over-subscribed, but always worthy of investigation die to access to start-up grants or loans on favourable terms. For example, some offer as much as £20,000 investment with no repayment clauses, but it's in exchange for 10% of the company. Either way, a worthwhile option.

Key Benefits

Think of incubator and accelerator programs as far more than low cost offices. Especially for people who are young or who have never run a business, the key advantages include:

O Free or discounted office space;

O Core infrastructure such as IT networks;

O Mentoring and coaching;

O Business plan development;

O Intensive training courses;

O Access to an established investor network;

O Access to a strong public relations outlet;

O Extensive business networking opportunities;

<u>Reducing Office Overheads</u>

The costs of commercial office or manufacturing space is one of the more daunting challenges when establishing a business. How can these be managed? Assuming you positively cannot launch operations using your home, what are some of the key considerations?

Take Only What You Require

Visions of packed meeting rooms can wait. When starting out, don't contract to any more space than is essential for your operations. You can move without much pain once the business is established.

With any facility, if clients will be visiting, you will want to make a good first impression. By starting with the smallest possible facility you can limit your 'fit-out' expenditure proportionately.

Shared Space

Consider co-working offices, which tend to be open-plan or with options for private rooms. You pay only for what you use, so if you have a client meeting you can book the well-equipped conference room by the hour. Such facilities often include telephone handling, and all manner of back office services such as printing and photocopying. With no long term commitments, this approach is ideal for the consulting-based start-up.

Serviced offices have dramatic variations of quality and cost, but they do offer flexible commitments. The space is yours to use as you wish, and you can fit your required infrastructure.

The small manufacturer / fabricator can start up with minimal requirements. Once you've scoured the local press and agencies, drive around industrial areas and look for a warehouse, factory or even a farm with idle space. The accountants of that business might be most amenable to a small rental income.

Leasing

Be very wary of the terms of a commercial lease, even more so if you are sub-leasing. The most common pitfall is the obligation at the end of the contract to revert the property to its original condition. This trap can prove to be a catastrophic expense.

Don't accept statements that 'this is the going rate'. With so much vacant commercial property, there's always a better option.

The start-up may be well served by entering into a license rather than a lease. With minimal contract durations, the license provides flexibility should you outgrow your space. Conversely, your business lacks security of tenure.

In your lease negotiation, do endeavour to secure a 'rent free' period. Depending upon the length of your projected lease, this can equate to the first six months – or longer – being rent-free: a bonus for your cash flow.

Location

Too many start-ups place undue emphasis upon their location. Unless you need a high-footfall retail location, don't pay for it.

Ease of access to clients is important, but the advantages for the modern technology business mean that more and more revenue is generated independently from the location: e-Commerce and video conferencing being but two changes.

Impact on Investors

As an investor yourself, you have an absolute desire to not see your profits go on 'bricks and mortar'. The same holds true for external investors. Your premises may be essential, but your focus should be upon your cash flow forecasts. Don't think an investor will not appreciate a conservative expenditure on premises.

People as a Service?

More than the financial burden of an office, the start-up is hampered from the outset with the massive overhead of paying staff salaries. There is another approach: Outsourcing.

Outsourcing does not mean exporting jobs to India and the Philippines, although it's possible. It means doing what almost every small business does: subcontracting work out to specialists, paying for what you use. We do this with lawyers and accountants, PR agencies and graphics designers. Your outsourced worker could be down the road, in Scotland or somewhere in Europe.

As a start-up or fledgling enterprise, nothing can impact your cash flow and profitability more positively than controlling your internal labour costs. It's obvious.

Cost of Employees

First though, let's establish the cost of an employee: the burden on the employer for a 'back office' administrator is generally in the order of 50%. Of this, 30% is from the obvious fixed overheads such as employer National Insurance Contributions, vacation time and benefits.

Role	Salary	Overheads	Annual Cost
HR Administrator	£18,000	£10,260	£28,260
Marketing Administrator	£19,000	£10,830	£29,830
Sales Administrator	£18,000	£10,260	£28,260
Bookkeeper	£21,000	£11,970	£32,970

The added hidden costs include such factors as the cost of their office space, IT infrastructure, software licenses, the rise in insurance premiums, utilities, and so forth.

Management Perspective: Finance

A 2014 survey by OVUM revealed that 75% of companies cited reducing labour costs as a key objective. This percentage increased to 86% for finance departments.

Just as the sole objective of a company is to increase its value for the shareholders, a core function of a Chief Financial Officer (CFO) is to seek to control costs of business processes and to maximise the profitability of the company. To put it more bluntly: it is not the mission of a company to employ people it doesn't require.

The Accounts Payable (AR) and Accounts Receivable (AP) are two processes which are easy to outsource. Businesses have been doing so for three centuries! With the advent of modern technologies, the sharing of data can be instantaneous – including paper based documentation. Further, the processes themselves for these two accounting functions are clear and precise: this enables a company to hand the work to a third party and have the process executed in a methodical and measurable fashion.

For the CFO, the up-front gains may be realised in fewer in-house staff, freeing up office space, reducing 'housing' costs and a lessened middle management workload. Typically, the measurable savings will be in the order of 40 – 55% of the total payroll and overhead. With that savings perhaps the 'Temp' worker won't be needed from 'the agency' next week, the parent on maternity / paternity leave won't need to be covered by an agency worker.

For the SME, the UK based National Outsourcing Association (NOA) reports that this sector will outsource ever more of their processes. According to the Engineers Employers Federation, 95% of businesses report significant price pressure from overseas vendors with a lower cost base.

Management Perspective: HR

The CIPD report, *HR Outsourcing and the HR Function,* revealed that the three leading reasons cited by UK based HR departments for outsourcing were access to skills & knowledge, quality and cost reduction.

> *PwC state that 'H.R. functions cost the average company £1,700 annually per employee'*

PricewaterhouseCoopers (PwC) reports that in-house administration of Human Resources has a cost of ownership 32% higher when fulfilling all tasks than delivered through external suppliers. Also, PwC state that H.R. functions costs the average company £1,700 annually per employee.

Payroll, and the reimbursement of expenses, are two clear processes which may cause conflict: if paid late or inaccurately then employee relations sour quickly. Some of the most easily addressed applications for outsourcing in HR departments include:

1. Payroll
2. Benefits administration
3. Legal services
4. Workforce administration

What Can You Outsource?

As you create your business plan, you might be shocked by the realisation that sales must escalate faster than planned simply to be able to afford to stay in business. Your cash flow and reserves are punished by staffing costs.

Do you need a receptionist? What about a marketing person? Probably! But will you have enough work to keep them fully occupied? Using a business process outsourcing firm means that you can use the required staff 'on demand', not paying for ide time.

Outsourcing means also that your occasional requirements may be fulfilled by a dedicated contractor. Here are some examples of the roles which a start-up can outsource to great effect:

○ IT services (especially helpdesk)

○ Call handling, telesales & lead generation

○ Customer service

○ Human resources & recruitment

○ Graphic and webpage design

○ Data management

○ Client relationship management

○ Web & application development

How does it Work?

An outsourcing company will work with you to define the job specification, skill sets required, working hours and so forth. They will go to the market and find job candidates, much like a recruitment agency.

You interview and select your staff and they become dedicated to you. In almost all respects they are your employee, taking your direction, training, fulfilling their tasks and working to your goals.

The difference lies in that they are employees of the outsourcing firm. Their office requirements, HR needs, taxes, payroll – everything – are the responsibility of the outsourcing company.

you see your total annual costs per employee drop from £30,000 to as little as £12,000 …

As an entrepreneur, you benefit from a single monthly payment for that person. No added overhead, no obligations and complete flexibility to add or reduce the staffing numbers according to your needs.

Because the outsourcing companies have bases in lower cost regions – whether Scotland or somewhere in Europe – you see your total annual costs per employee drop from £30,000 to as little as £12,000. This is too great of an advantage to overlook.

In the sample business plan at the back of this book, you will see how outsourcing changes completely the economics and ultimate viability of the business.

Maximising Service Revenue

To what extent does your business model include revenue forecasts for Professional Services? If you're from the IT industry, you will know exactly what is being asked: services ancillary to the product being sold, such as installation, configuration, documentation, training, service and support.

Such services can account for 25% of total revenue, and while there is a cost overhead in terms of manpower, the margins are entirely satisfactory. Of considerable importance too, is the activities delivered reveal further sales opportunities and improve client retention.

The impact of people-centric business is revealed in valuations. Accenture, the global consulting giant, trades at 1.6x earnings, whereas a software company in the SaaS space will typically have a valuation in the order of 12x revenues. It doesn't matter: 50% margin is positive income.

How does the SME – regardless of sector – offer more services to their client base? Why? First and foremost, think of services as the single most important means of maximising client retention. From there, one expects referrals, and an introduction is by far the least expensive form of client acquisition.

Professional Services need not be limited only to software companies. As an example, in the ideal world, a creative agency will not just conceive a business name, brand, logo and colour scheme, but they will take the entire process through all approvals. They will leverage their 'might' to achieve this to defined standards, with a fast turn-around and minimal engagement from yourself. The reality is many just sell you the logo etc. and leave it up to you to get it licensed and trademarked.

Identifying service based revenue should be integral to any business plan. The more one entwines your deliverable with the client, the more likely you are to remain the de facto supplier.

Subscription Services

Whether one looks at Software as a Service (SaaS) or Product as a Service (PaaS), this field is becoming critical as customers migrate towards new business models which enable them to pay only for what they actually consume.

As you design and review your business plan, consider if these new approaches have bearing upon your product offering, and how you approach your business in general.

Software as a Service (SaaS)

The surest way to upset a car dealer is to walk in with cash. The salesperson might be overjoyed, but the folks in the back office will not be smiling: they would have hoped to double their profit via your loan interest payments.

It's much the same with software. Software as a Service involves the online rental of software, typically freeing you, the client, from any costs associated with buying and maintaining a server. Not only that, but to access the software you pay only a small monthly and all of your maintenance is included.

For the client this is fantastic news. The SME, anxious to preserve cash, can have access to software which might recently have had an upfront purchase cost of many £1,000's and yet now be paying a small monthly service fee.

For the software vendor, they too are smiling. The can predict their revenues, and they know that they can expect the number of licenses you require to increase. You will be back.

The business model works. Variations are offered across industry, from Microsoft and Apple, to Amazon and Netflix. As will be detailed in the sample business plan included here, a recurring service contract can transform your sales model, with the benefits of contract renewals propelling growth far beyond the old 'sell it once' approach.

Product as a Service (PaaS)

Industrial equipment can be offered on a pay-per-use basis similar to the Software as a Service. The concept is simple enough: to transform the product from one which is standalone to one which integrates the product with a service offering.

> *"IDC Manufacturing Insights estimates that 40% of Top 100 discrete manufacturers and 20% of Top 100 process manufacturers will provide product as service platforms by 2018"*

It's happened with the ubiquitous office photocopier, to offer but one example. Customers are freed from significant up-front capital expenditures, while the manufacturers gain a continuous service revenue stream. For both customer and manufacturer, there's the added service advantage.

In the case of the humble photocopier, they now include sensors and data metrics gathering software which pre-orders replacement toner, detects usage rates to forecast service intervals and even reports usage patterns and costs. The net result is that clients can experience greatly enhanced service from their supplier which can actually reduce the cost of the product still further.

The Dutch electronics giant, Philips, made changes to its lighting division, a field in which they're the leaders. In a drive to reduce waste from light bulbs they changed their business model on its head: they introduced a lighting service: they offer lighting as a series of services such as advisory (evaluation), project services (creation and implementation), lifecycle services (performance, maintenance).

It boils down to answering the question as to whether the client wants the product itself or just the benefit it brings to their lives? If your business is to be engaged in creating a physical product, what new ways might be conceived which would enable you to take it to market in a new format?

As with renting a car, you don't want to own that car, you just require use if it in a particular location. In return for the convenience of receiving the car (with its service included), you are equally prepared to pay a premium price.

The process of change has barely begun. Already, architects are creating buildings in which the component parts are tagged for re-use. The field of recycling is being forced to grow due to new regulations. Such initiatives are pushing businesses to conceive of how their products can be incorporated with services and taken to market in new ways. Can yours?

Client Acquisition in the Digital Age

- *Your Marketing Plan*
- *Your Website: Will you be Found?*
- *The Importance of Website Interaction*
- *The Relevance of Social Media*
- *Capturing the Global Marketplace*
- *Leveraging e-Commerce*

Your Marketing Plan

How many times has your mind drifted towards going it alone? Perhaps you have felt frustrated that your ideas, initiatives and hard work are under-appreciated? For the sake of argument, it matters not whether you are an engineer or a photocopier salesperson, a programmer or a musician: you have an idea and you want to strike out on your own and create a new business, knowing you are talented in your field.

Your idea takes shape and, along the way, you realise you require a business plan. Alone or with a friend or two you set to work and prepare the rather formulaic documents, perhaps seeking input from someone versed in finance to structure the numbers.

> *most business people have little idea of the complexities of implementing a modern marketing approach*

Like so many before you, the maximum effort goes into the profit and loss (P&L) and the cash flow forecasts.

It's not a bad start, but what of the marketing plan? Unless you have experience in marketing it is unlikely you realise all that is entailed, and it's not an exaggeration to suggest that most business people have little idea of the complexities of implementing a modern marketing approach.

No matter your skill as a tradesman, your financial wizardly, technical or creativity, what hope is there for your business if you open your doors (either brick and mortar or a digital presence) and nobody knows you're there?

Marketing drives business. Indeed, it's so fundamental that to bury it as some form of afterthought is to risk your entire venture. Sadly, too many businesses have failed because the owners are thinking of what they knew from twenty years ago and not recognising the world of today. As just one example, almost every book on writing a business plan still refer to the printing and postage of brochures as a fundamental cost, a topic which has desperately little relevance in today's marketplace.

Your Website: Will you be Found?

Within the context of writing a business plan, it is appropriate to explore how the business will ensure its presence on the internet: after all, this will undoubtedly affect the success of your sales and marketing plan.

Knowing in advance that you have a strategy may affect how you write the plan itself. Perhaps there are aspects of e-Commerce you might think to include, no matter how simple, which could enhance your commercial reach?

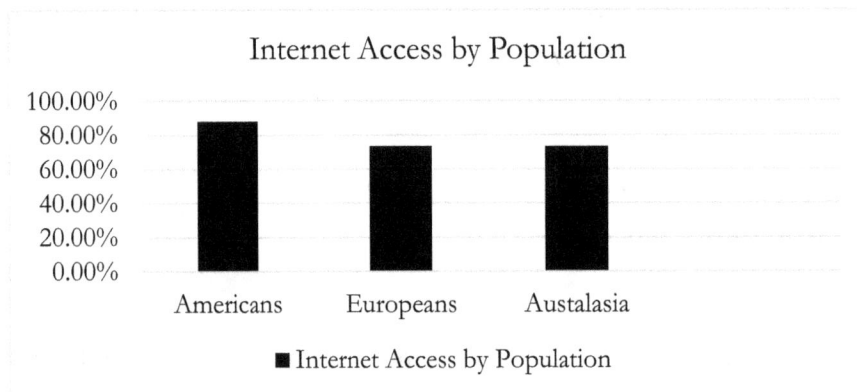

Internet Access by Population

	Americans	Europeans	Austalasia
Internet Access by Population	~85%	~72%	~73%

■ Internet Access by Population

As to those in certain professions who think the internet doesn't affect them, they need to remember that 75% of all internet users live in the top twenty countries (ranked by size of economy). Every business needs a refined internet presence to capture the more than 70% of their likely customer base (see chart below).

The Need for Speed!

With ever improving broadband access speeds, the average internet user has become highly demanding: instant gratification is their priority. The upshot is that even a delay of just one second can cause an 11% drop in traffic to your site. The American retail giant, Walmart, released a study which showed they gain a staggering 11% increase in revenue for every 100ms (millisecond) improvement in website speed.

In 2015, the average webpage took five seconds to load and contained 3MB of data. Anything more than this is unacceptable, but your target should be for pages to load in three seconds. Test your website with Google Page Insights, and explore the range of alternative testing sites too, with Pingdom being a market leader.

You might elect to use a WordPress site – that is a website based upon any number of free or inexpensive templates. The advantage of WordPress is mostly the low cost of 'going live' and access to a vast array of 'plug-ins' which add functionality at very low cost.

The disadvantages of WordPress include:

○ Often slower than 'hard coded' sites;

○ Gimmicky, and often highly graphics intensive;

○ Adjusting to 'your' look and feel is not always easy or cheap;

If your budget permits, opting to have a website programmed from scratch ('hard coded'), leaves you in total control. Apart from being able to achieve the fastest page-load times, your clients will recognise that this is a unique site. For some, that is a quality statement of relevance.

Search Engine Optimisation (SEO) Basics

Since the early days of search engine design, the task consisted of building a database of all words on any webpage and displaying the pages in order according to which pages matched the search term with the most 'hits'. These words came to be defined as keywords, so if a firm was selling a television, they would list brand names on their website also.

The process has changed a lot. Search engines are now designed to examine relevance to the user, and with powerful software it's not just having enough relevant words on the page but entire phrases.

Staying relevant has become a challenge for the SME, generally lacking in sophisticated marketing expertise. It's not enough to tell a website developer to make an attractive site, that same developer must be given the information required to ensure that the pages will be found.

The business team must define the keywords which will attract clients and also define a 'basket' of related terms. This is the beginning of the process known as Search Engine Optimisation, or SEO for short.

Google will be examining your website for high quality information and relevance to the searches made by their users. To overcome the dirty tricks of old, the software is now looking at those keywords within the context of the quality of the text and other data which surrounds them.

A top-level objective for the new business, therefore, is to consider the key words and key phrases your potential clients will use to find your business.

The next fundamental is the existence and quality of links to your website. It's now not just a matter of there being links, but to establish links from 'higher quality' websites. An example would be if your website has a link from a major newspaper, then it is given a higher credibility than a link from a friend's blog. The assumption is simple: the major newspaper has more sites linking to it, and from it, and therefore is given a higher trust rating.

it is a mission-critical exercise to define the keywords and key phrases which will be relevant to your potential client base

The final part of this introduction to SEO is that your website is also rated according to user behaviour while on your site. Engagement – or what the user actually does while on your site – is of great importance. Evaluation of how much time each visitor spends on your site, how many pages they review, how much time do they invest, do they share it via social media … these are all important.

As you delve deeper into this field you will read about 'bounce rate'. This refers to the rate at which users click through from a search result, take a look, and then 'bounce back' to the search engine results. Your goal, unsurprisingly, is to reduce the percentage who do just that and to get them to stay on your webpages and to interact.

As you prepare to launch your business, it is a mission-critical exercise to define the keywords and key phrases which will be relevant to your potential client base and to structure both your product portfolio and marketing efforts to maximise exposure.

Content: The Magic Ingredient

As noted above, Google has re-engineered their algorithms to 'understand' content. As an example, if you are selling tangible products such as 'camping equipment', then you might have a webpage which lists a tent for sale.

You could describe the tent with the manufacturer's name, product number, material, weight, dimensions and capacity. That's simple enough, but the search engines will recognise that you have added nothing special: there's no quality or originality.

Bearing in mind the SEO objectives too, you might extend the description with some text you have written in-house. In this case, you might include sentences which include: 'a superior-grade lightweight tent for the backpacker because …' and, 'best protection from rain and snow because …'. Your content is thus reflecting exact phrases which a prospective customer might be using.

Continuing with this theme, once your product descriptions are all customised and enhanced, how might you foster engagement? How can you reduce 'bounce backs'? Well, you know a lot about camping and tents in general, so write an article. Whatever you do, make it original and don't copy and paste from somewhere else (such as from the manufacturer) since Google's software is sophisticated enough to recognise such tricks.

Your goal should be to create articles of 500 – 1,500 words in length on topics related to your business overall. Plan your strategy to encourage engagement, so think of how and why people might want to share your article via Social Media. Think: is this shareable?

Content themes may include leading words such as:

○ Five ways to …

○ 10 advantages of …

○ The six best …

○ The three-minute guide to …

○ User Review of …

A caution, though, is to make sure you don't just churn out writing. The sting in the tail for content is that the search engines identify 'idle' content, and if your site has too many pages which are unshared this can lessen your rankings. Questions to ask about each page include:

○ Why is a reader likely to share this piece?

○ Will readers be tempted to add comments?

○ Are there irritating advertisements which deter readers?

○ Are there enough key words and key phrases?

Supplemental content which can boost your success includes manuals, how-to guides, technical White Papers, regional overviews, infographics, podcasts and videos.

Mobile Users

Addressing the needs of the mobile phone user is now 'mission critical'. Consider these statistics from 2015: 78% of the world's population has a mobile phone and 46% have access to the internet.

Almost 70% of all mobile phones in Europe and the United States are Smartphones and the consequent impact on marketing has been massive: in 2015 Google announced that searches via mobiles outnumbered searches via personal computers.

Displaying a website on a mobile phone in a user-friendly fashion is essential, and the industry term coined for handling the dynamic shift to different platforms is 'responsiveness'.

With mobile users now representing the bulk of Google searches, Google reacted by changing their search algorithms further. The result is that websites which don't offer 'responsive' layouts are penalised, with non-responsive websites securing much lower rankings.

As you develop your strategic marketing plan, it is paramount that you start with the stipulation that your website shall be responsive.

The Importance of Website Interaction

Even in 2016, too many businesses treat their website as something akin to a digital newspaper advertisement. I'm referring to all of the sites which lack any customer engagement and just broadcast products alongside some minimal blurb.

Enhancing the Greeting

When a client enters your shop or office, your staff surely greet them, setting the stage for establishing an initial client relationship. The immediate follow-through is the simple offer of assistance to answer questions, locate product or find a particular specialist. Once greeted positively, and finding a pleasant environment, the customer is less likely to turn on their heels and leave. How will your website achieve this?

Whether one enters a tyre shop or the office of a law firm, following the greeting there is an offer such as a cup of coffee which conveys a welcome and an invitation to linger. Unlike in your shop or office the client can vanish from your website in an instant, and thus we see the digital version of that cup of coffee: knowledge for free.

The knowledge is most typically in the form of a PDF document or an e-Book. Whether two pages or twenty, if this offer is accepted then the client engagement has begun. There's a further analogy to the physical world: the servicing of coffee also involves introductions, an exchange of names. Your website should do this with the when offering the free information by a simple request for the client's email address.

We shall explore the collection of email addresses further.

Appointment Creation

Automating appointment creation saves your own time and resources. Whether it's to schedule a fifteen-minute telephone chat, or an hour of service or consultancy, why would you not offer this if at all applicable to your business?

A particular advantage is that the client fully expects to provide substantial additional information about themselves and their requirements. The integration of this function with your contact management system is normally very easy.

The Blog as your Conversation Piece

In almost any field, conversation with clients, whether potential or existing, is a fundamental aspect of the entire customer relations process. It might range from picking your brains for advice or comment to exploring a client's exact requirements. Conversation opens the door for you to position your business as credible suppliers.

As the saying goes, 'people buy from people'. This holds true in e-Commerce, including even shoppers on Amazon and eBay who review seller's ratings and credentials.

Your website needs a blog, and it's for you to decide upon the form. It might offer pieces on products, industry insights, your innovations, 'tips and tricks', or a multitude of other information but it must exist. This is your conversation piece.

Interaction is what creates the conversation, so enable the function which allows reader comments. You have the option to screen these before publication or not, although the general recommendation is for screening.

Apart from boosting your presence in the search engine results, with every blog comment you will add an email address to your marketing database.

Live Chat: Get the Engagement Started

In specialist retail, a client will decide within thirty seconds whether they are inclined to purchase. It's even more hazardous with the internet where your client is perhaps more than a little lost, uncertain of what they need, unsure if you have 'it' and spoiled for choice as to where to look next. Their consequence of this nervousness is that they will leave your site before buying anything. If only you had talked to them!

Think of Live Chat as having a salesperson within reach, not interrupting but always available: a shop floor presence which eludes most websites. Of course, it remains an invaluable tool for delivering technical support services too, but it's moved far beyond. How powerful is it? A study conducted by Shopify showed that customers engaged with a live chat representative were three times more likely to become return shoppers and averaged an increase of 48% in their average order sizes. This is surely revenue which mustn't be missed!

Your Live Chat service might be offered via a link or a 'pop up', but for many the latter is by far the most effective. Interestingly, your business doesn't have to be vast to provide Live Chat services. You might be able to allocate one or two of your back office staff to the task, but very often, a Business Process Outsourcing (BPO) provider can provide basic service for a small monthly cost. The possibilities are unlimited, and for some businesses it's the Live Chat which drives successful sales.

Tell your Friends

The use of the internet is generally a solitary occupation, yet it's human nature to want to share experiences. If your product is within a niche, then the odds are that any single customer will have friends with similar needs or desires – and simply by adding a few of the popular social media sharing buttons your website gives those customers a chance to tell their friends what they've found. People might buy from people, but nothing beats a personal recommendation.

At a minimum, your website should offer sharing functions for Facebook and Twitter, but add Pinterest and Digg links if you have images or videos.

Every social media sharing option builds your marketing opportunity, especially if you create a presence on the applicable platforms.

Subscribe Me!

The pinnacle of website engagements, subscribers to your website are your hottest prospects: they've asked you to interrupt their days to tell them about new information, products, services, opinions and more. Cultivate them carefully.

Apart from anting to follow your blog, clients might be tempted to subscribe to an email broadcast as to when new products are available, timely information about a specific topic of interest, or just a general curiosity about your offering.

Ensure you maintain your marketing database to indicate subscribers since these are your strongest potential clients. The information you send to them must be carefully measured for timing, content and anticipated action.

The Follow Through

People are creatures of habit, and everyone likes to be heard. So for every customer for whom you have an email address, why not send a one-time customer survey questionnaire?

Just a few questions, a promise that it takes less than thirty seconds to complete, and a link through to your website and, you've re-engaged. Your email might reference a new product but that's not important: every click through increases the chances of generating repeat business.

Video Chat and Online Meetings

Software vendors, specialist retailers, consultants, lawyers and countless others can present their products and services quickly and efficiently through video meetings. The technology is available for free or, for the more sophisticated options which support large groups of invitees, for a relatively small costs – just take a look at Skype, LiveMeeting, GoToMeeting and others.

For the professions and those involved in business to business sales, the cost saving can be dramatic. A solicitor can offer a brief initial consultation, or the software salesperson can evaluate the client's core requirements without the time and expense of travel. Moreover, one can screen and evaluate the client's needs and likelihood of their becoming a client.

There is, still, a perceived loss of 'human interaction', but ruthless use of one's time for client acquisition is mandatory.

Host a Webinar

Many potential clients will subscribe to a webinar, an online presentation or talk on a vast range of subjects. Typically, one-directional, the presenter can use all manner of media and not be reliant of dull PowerPoint presentations.

As a presenter, you see exactly which of your prospective clients logged-in, and this gives you a focus: put your further effort towards these prospects as they have pre-qualified themselves.

The Relevance of Social Media

According to The Chartered Institute of marketing, the average cost of acquiring a new customer is seven times more than the cost of retention. Notwithstanding that so many businesses invest nothing in customer retention, those which do understand the importance use Social Media as a means of achieving this while controlling the cost.

Social Media helps to create loyalty. It may be deployed in various ways to deliver support, communication and active engagement. Whether you use Social Media in your personal life or not, a growing proportion of your clients regard it as important and expect you to have a presence.

While the number of Social Media channels continues to grow, marketing departments are becoming more focussed since the time and effort to manage and maintain the presence is recognised as a burden. Learn from the largest users, and deliver a superior customer experience by concentrating on outstanding presence on just a few core channels.

For a business selling to consumers, the key candidates are Facebook, Twitter, and Google +. The same applies to business to business vendors, but with the addition of a LinkedIn presence.

Channels such as YouTube and Instagram are generally only of secondary importance and are best deployed when the core platforms are well established.

The above takes on significant importance in light of Google's changes to their algorithms: a key factor affecting your search result rankings is the extent to which you share, link and engage. Without even entering the field of paid-for rankings, use of Social Media is the single most effective tool to help your business to be found.

Facebook

The Facebook social media platform offers you an audience of 1.23 billion active users each month. As an advertiser, you can distil the user-base by region, age, sex, interests and other characteristics.

The age group of 18 – 34 year olds represents 64% of all Facebook users, and ages 35-54 account for 29% of all users. Clearly, the ability to target advertising at one's core customer base demographics is remarkable.

You might spend £10 on an advertisement to have it viewed by 2,000 people, but if they are all known to be generally interested in your product or service then the effects of your precision marketing are greatly enhanced. Such tools also enable very affordable test marketing campaigns.

Twitter

If Facebook is the leader in terms of sheer numbers of users, then Twitter is the leader in terms of volume of messages, with more than 500 million 'tweets' sent every day.

As a marketer, you are interested in those social messages referencing your organisation or product.

The volume of 'tweets' makes it the very best platform for use as a customer service and business development channel. Monitor the network and give instant customer service interaction.

LinkedIn

Used by the business to business vendor, LinkedIn has a network of more than 330 million users, and they tend to approach the platform with a business engagement outlook.

With the LinkedIn social media marketing options, you can broadcast your messages directly to the working user, and so build relationships you're your future customers.

Google+

Google+ is of rising importance to any business. Once you have developed a strong presence on the site, any user of Google will be presented with a snippet of your business profile on their results pages.

Pay attention to Google+ Communities. These offer superior client targeting options and by sharing your content you can pinpoint your audience exactly.

Leveraging e-Commerce

e-Commerce is about far more than offering a product online and having clients buy it, with perhaps only minimal interaction on the part of your business. Of course that's wonderful, but what of the brand-building and customer experience?

Your efforts to create a brand for your company must never be dismissed. Invest continuous effort in ensuring the cumulative experience for every client is positive and that it encourages them to return.

Maximise the Return Rate

A book in its own right, but start thinking about how your business can improve the customer's experience when visiting your e-Commerce site. Here are a few thoughts to get you started:

- ○ Offer a pop-up 'Live Chat' option. This is something which can be run during office hours only or 24x7.

- ○ Remove the checkout registration process. Faced with a long form or just reverting to another vendor, the client has only to make one click. Offering a guest registration while you accept their payment details is much friendlier.

- ○ Offer a detailed Frequently Asked Questions page: surveys show that online customers prefer to be self-sufficient.

- ○ Refine your email messages to become something memorable.

Explore New Channels

For many retailers, the advantages of eBay and Amazon are profound. Not only might a specific product be sold, but your very presence exposes your business and e-Commerce site.

Consumers are becoming more astute. If they find a product online or in your physical store they are more tempted than ever to go to the Amazon website and compare prices, availability and shipping costs. Maintaining a presence on Amazon, eBay and other such sites is now a mission critical requirement for many businesses. This approach is referred to as 'multi-channel selling', as it relies upon a multi-merchant system.

Facebook, Twitter, and other social media platforms realise the significant revenue opportunities and businesses must be prepared to adapt if they want to grow their market share.

Affiliate Marketing

Across a vast array of products, from car rentals to training courses, manufacturers to automobile servicing, the use of Affiliate Marketing is growing exponentially.

Affiliate marketing may be defined as a form marketing through which a business 'rewards one or more affiliates for each visitor or customer brought by the affiliate's own marketing efforts'.

Almost regardless of what you are selling, if your product or service could be marketed by an online business for a small percentage, then surely it's worth rewarding the third party for the reduced client acquisition costs?

Affiliate marketers vary considerably in their quality, and the majority of their traffic is generated via SEO (79%) and social media (60%). As a subset of your overall e-Commerce marketing effort, you should seek out a select few affiliates and stay focused on your niche.

In terms of pure advertising, your obligation is to recognize the source of your website visitors and compensate the affiliate accordingly. As a small business, this can relieve you of significant time, energy and expense.

Many affiliate programs enable third parties to resell your product, but the actual sale is made via your e-Commerce site. When the customer seeks to buy the product they are linked through to your e-Commerce platform for you to complete the order processing and fulfillment. Payment to the affiliate is then in the form of a commission.

Don't expect this approach to transform your business, but even if only a few percent of your revenue is achieved by this mechanism, then it must be advantageous.

For more information, the CJ Affiliate by Conversant (formerly Commission Junction) is the leading global affiliate marketing network, operating across the United States and Europe.

Part Two

A step-by-step guide

- *22 typical business plan mistakes*
- *The creative process*
- *Start writing, step-by step*

22 Typical Business Plan Mistakes

1. An Executive Summary which fails to inspire. It must captivate the investor and answer their key questions.

2. Unrealistic growth forecasts. Few start-ups with £100,000 capital are going to achieve £2m revenue within three years.

3. Sloppy appearance: lacking a cover page and table of contents, printed onto cheap photocopy paper secured with a staple.

4. Plans which includes neither secured customers nor marketing research.

5. No provision for Directors salaries: if they won't be taking cash out of the business, then how will they survive?

6. Use of hyperbole, such as 'no risk', 'fool-proof' and 'guaranteed'. All investments have risk, and your business is no different.

7. Using phrases which are mere hype 'to become an industry leader', or broad unsubstantiated statements such as 'It is a known fact that …'

8. Claims of being 'unique' or 'without competition'. CEO's of 45% of large start-ups cited 'product not wanted' as their primary reason for business failure.

9. The 'hockey stick' revenue growth forecast in which revenue shoots skyward at some future point.

10. Lazy, and generally inaccurate, cash flow projections.

11. Vague or muddled English, spelling mistakes, poor grammar, typographical errors, needless repetition.

12. Marketing-speak such as 'proactive', or waffle such as 'at this point in time'.

13. Techno-babble and acronyms deter investors. Write in a style suitable for an educated layman.

14. Appearing to lack a business focus: you cannot be all things to all people. Define your niche and think of four products vs. twenty.

15. Too long! A business plan should not exceed forty pages, and some might only require ten pages. Move excess detail to the appendices.

16. Plans which lack specific, measurable objectives.

17. Lacking in research. The plan must convey a strong sense of expertise.

18. Illegible financial projections. Always print these onto A3 paper and have them professionally folded into your business plan.

19. Blasé risk analysis: don't hide the risks from yourself or the investor.

20. Embedding an exit strategy into a start-up plan reeks both of a lack of commitment and of an uncomfortable arrogance.

21. Seeking funds which are not clearly intended for business growth.

22. Asking for investment without offering reasonable share ownership commensurate with the risk.

The Creative Process

- *How to Start*
- *Presentation Guidelines*

How to Start

First and foremost, remember that this is your business plan: the content should be entirely the same whether you are looking for any outside investment or not. After all, if you feel the need to 'fluff it up', then you are admitting to yourself that there are risks and uncertainties which you've not yet resolved. Your own time, money and reputation is at risk, as well perhaps as your career and financial security.

What then are the guiding principles?

○ Absolute honesty

○ Cautious optimism

○ Objectivity

○ Accurate and believable financials

Length

There's no absolute, but no SME should require a business plan of more than 40 pages, and few can be condensed to less than 20 pages unless it is truly an encapsulation, a five page long 'first look'.

By all means create a quick overview: five pages distilled from your master document This is only likely to be of use as a teaser for a potential investor who requests a summary. This shortened version is of no use to you otherwise, and it should consist of the Executive Summary, Business Overview and the Financials.

Presentation

Your plan must be easy to read quickly, and it must be attractive. The cover page differentiates the careless from the professional, and it demands clear information as to the name of the business and the key contact information. By all means use a graphic.

The Table of Contents is an absolute pre-requisite, and it is for you to ensure the accuracy. Your plan will have undergone numerous revisions by the time it's completed, and updating this table can prove problematic for those not intimately familiar with MS-Word.

Beware of acronyms. If you write that you are going to be selling to 'C-Level', what of the reader unfamiliar with the term? If you mean CEO then say it. If indeed your industry or technology is jargon intensive, then offer a glossary. That doesn't let you off the hook though: the investors might be interested in the bottom line and not wanting a crash course in the actual technology. The essence is to write for professionals who might know little or nothing of your niche.

Use lots of 'white space'. If your text is cramped, then it's a daunting read which may mean that much is ignored or merely skimmed. Spread it out! If the consequence is an extra five pages overall, then so be it. Use page breaks liberally so sections are properly divided.

Avoid flabby prose. Phrases such as 'at the end of the day', 'at this point in time', add nothing and might cause irritation to the reader.

Avoid stating the obvious. Of course you want 'to become the market leader' ... why else would you be starting the business?

O   Bullet points have impact. Easy to read quickly.

Your financial projections will come in for a lot of scrutiny. It's off-putting to see a plan based upon a £100,000 investment project a turnover of £3m within just two or three years. If you make such claims, then offer significant explanation.

Consider using an accountant to prepare your financial projections. Unless finance is your forte, then the objectivity of a professional is money well spent. You will probably recoup the cost many times over through being made aware of tax, grants, and other mechanisms which will help your business grow. Any investor will note the professionalism of the data too, and this further improves your outlook. Regardless, you owe it to yourself to have your projections verified.

Coloured charts convey a lot of information in a form the reader may assimilate quickly. They help the memory, too, so your plan might stand out from the rest. Stick to two dimensional bar charts and pie charts unless unavoidable. A stacked Bar chart is useful to differentiate sales by market segment, for example. Remember to keep the source numbers close to the chart or indicate in which appendix they may be found, and always reference any chart or table in the body text.

take your plan to a graphics designer and have the layout polished by a professional

Don't be a font fool: not more than three fonts should be used, with the key sans serif fonts being Ariel or Verdana. For a more traditional look use serif fonts such as Times New Roman or Century. Keep all body text to 11 or 12-point font sizes. If you are seeking investors, then take your plan to a graphics designer and have the layout polished by a professional. Students designers are only too willing to undertake simple projects such as this. It's well worth the moderate expense.

Always print in colour on the highest quality paper (a minimum of 100gsm weight). Very stiff pages, such as 250gsm paper, convey a sense of quality, with a light cream colour conveying wealth and success. It should go without saying but the final result must be spiral bound. Sadly, many plans I've seen are black and white prints held together by a staple and, consequently, are anything but inspiring.

A Step by Step Guide

There are eight sections to the business plan, presented in a logical sequence to entice the reader. Subsections to these eight may be added as required.

Section One:	*The Introduction*
Section Two:	*The Business*
Section Three:	*Market Overview*
Section Four:	*Competition*
Section Five:	*Sales & Marketing*
Section Six:	*Operations*
Section Seven:	*Financials*
Section Eight:	*Appendix*

The Example: Market Précis

A small business start-up with up to £120,000 of available capital from three business partners. They are self-funded by cash.

Jack Hamilton and his friends Lucy White and Jane Brown have worked alongside each other for five years. Jack is a 'sales machine' while Lucy is a marketing professional. They've become frustrated in their current employment and they've hit upon a business concept which is closely related to their current industry.

In going into business together, they are pooling their resources and they've agreed that they can each invest up to £40,000 via a combination of redundancy payments, home equity release, and cash savings.

They are writing their business plan in the hope to of raising further capital through friends and family or perhaps a Business Angel. They each have modest additional savings in the event further investment is required.

Section One: The Introduction

1.1 Executive Summary

The Executive Summary is a précis of both your concept and your business plan and it must captivate the reader from the outset. There is no part more critical: failure to properly articulate your idea and to summarise the financial objectives will condemn your efforts to the trash, unread.

To grab the attention of an investor, your writing has to be 'compact' and direct. You want money and the investor wants exact information. Simply put, you must deliver clear answers to the investor's six questions: *'What's the idea? Why will it succeed? How much cash? What's the risk? What's the ROI? When will it pay off?'*. Answer these well, and your Executive Summary is perfect.

From personal experience, I can say without exaggeration that an investor might glance at a hundred plans before reading past the Executive Summary and, even then, perhaps only for a brief look at the financial projections. Investors are busy people and highly selective. If they've not even met you, then your knowledge, charm and enthusiasm are redundant. So how do you tilt the odds in your favour?

Brevity! There is a growing tendency for consultants and writers for business magazines and blogs to suggest that the Executive Summary may be two pages in length. This is entirely wrong. There is no concept which should be beyond one's ability to summarise in 400 words. From an aesthetic perspective, one page of text in an attractive, easy to read, font conveys to the reader that you respect their time. In a split second the decision is made to invest a modicum of that time to absorb what you have to say. The two-page summary suggests you have no clear understanding of your proposal, no elevator pitch, no dynamism and no respect. Be succinct.

Precision! Having read the Executive Summary, the investor will glance next at the financial projections which, by convention, are always placed across the final pages of the business plan. It is imperative that the figures referenced in your text match the financial projections in the tables, and it remains shocking how often plans fail at this simple hurdle.

Without the plan itself, you cannot write the Executive Summary and, yet, this is where you begin nonetheless. Confused? I's actually obvious: you need a focal point on which everything you write, and all of your research centres.

Faced with a substantial creative project which, in all probability, is outside of your normal experience, define your focus now with a series of bullet points which answer the following four questions:

O What is the focus of the business?

O What is the product or service?

O What are the USP's?

O What is the target market?

The notes you make here will keep bringing you back to the basic question: *'is what I'm writing supporting why this business is a sound investment?'*. You might be surprised at how many drift off topic. Save this, don't edit it. Just keep adding notes below until the very end.

Throughout the rest of the process of writing your business plan you will be forced into critical thinking which will prompt profound adjustments to your initial assumptions. When the rest of the plan is complete you will marvel at how much changed. Refer back to these early notes at every stage.

Step by Step Guidance

Welcome back! You've completed every other section, and you've made countless edits. Your early notes are now obsolete and it is now time to write the Executive Summary: you're almost done. Remember the investor's six questions: *'What's the idea? Why will it succeed? How much cash? What's the risk? What's the ROI? When will it pay off?'* – let's put it together!

Approach your work by creating nine paragraphs as follows:

- ○ Start with the obvious: 'who we are and what we do'. Open with your company name and legal structure, then summarise the business itself as simply as possible. Refer to your elevator pitch.

- ○ What is the market demand you are fulfilling and what is your core value proposition? This must be explicit: it lies at the very heart of the entire exercise. Omission or woolliness will be spotted by any investor.

- ○ Offer a snapshot of the marketplace, competition and your sales. It is critical that start-up's must reference any secured or advanced sales.

- ○ The longest paragraph encapsulates your sales and marketing plan. Cover your top-level USP's first and then convey to the reader you're the business will achieve growth. Incorporate any justifications for your cash flow forecasts. Split into two paragraphs more than six lines.

- ○ Summarise the start-up investment, cite the FY1 revenues and result, followed by the full three year projected revenues and results.

- ○ Summarise how the business can generate cash. Detail the three-year ROI based upon investment vs. accumulated cash.

- ○ Prudence is a virtue. Offer examples as to how the business will be thrifty and how it shall live within its means under your leadership.

- ○ Who are the Directors? Are they experienced? What about their shareholding? To what extent are they investing?

- ○ The invitation. What is it you want? Close with a firm statement which invites inquisitiveness such as '… seeking investors who recognise the potential rewards and significant tax advantages'.

No matter how technically complex your product or service, your Executive Summary must use plain English. Complexities may be acceptable within the business plan, but not here.

Not everyone finds writing easy, and with the pressure of understanding the importance of this section, do remember to write fluidly. Don't fret if you fill two or three pages before you condense it down. Parsing text is generally easier than finding the perfect prose at the outset. This is where a specialist can assist.

Finally, test your Executive Summary on several people, especially if they are in business. They don't need to see the whole plan yet, but you need to measure their understanding and make adjustments accordingly. Revise your work until it's flawless.

1.2 Business Overview

Your reader will have had their interest piqued by your Executive Summary and they will probably have had a look at the Cash Flow forecast. In the Business Overview you get to be more expansive.

You are aiming to give a 'bird's eye view' of your business, addressing very much the scope of the product and services, how and where you will operate, and the nature of the market demand.

While a single page is preferred, extending to two full pages is perfectly acceptable for the Business Overview since this is one of the core narratives in your presentation. Remember, though, that so much text has no visual appeal and you are well advised to insert a prominent quotation or a colourful and informative chart to catch the reader's eye. Include either or both as is appropriate.

Step by Step Guidance

You might like to start by copying your opening for the Executive Summary, then rephrase it and elaborate further. Refer back to your 'three-minute elevator pitch', since this should have almost everything you need. Structure your paragraphs as follows:

○ What is the nature of your business and in what sector do you operate? Summarise your product or service in a few words and encapsulate who represents your target market.

○ Explain your product or service in more detail and close with your strongest value proposition. In our example, we state: 'Typically, a client producing in-house will spend >£50,000 per year but with Business Précis this overhead is reduced by 40%'.

○ Include a 'punchy' quotation.

○ Offer a market overview, detail 'the need' and close by explaining how you fulfil that need. While saving money is good, strive to define your second value proposition in terms which convey added value. This can be seen in our example: *'client acquisition rates grow by up to 40% and client retention is increased up to 70%.'*

○ How and where will you operate? Are you leasing a particular property? What are some of the key aspects of your business in terms of operations, staffing, efficiencies, management? Be short and to the point but do give it some 'life'.

○ Summarise your business feature with a series of not more than five bullet points. Include your vertical market focus and additional revenue models such as professional services, training or after-market service contracts.

○ 'The close': a good opportunity to summarise the Directors experience and involvement.

1.3 Summary of Products and Services

Encapsulate your core product offering and then explain what it will do to fulfil the needs of your clients. Try to avoid absolute repetition of what you wrote previously in the Executive Summary or Business Overview.

You use this section to summarise any key attributes of your product, by using statements such as 'it is fully developed and ready to go to market', or 'we have completed our prototype testing successfully and now seek a manufacturer'. If you are a software vendor, is the product in Alpha, Beta, or Release Candidate 1, 2, 3 etc.

Avoid trying to cram in too much detail. Remember, this part is a summary, so keep it to just that.

In the example business plan, the vendor has three products but only one is 'core'. It is reasonable to detail only this central offering.

Step by Step Guidance

This can be a tricky section to complete, so you might start by addressing the points below. Don't mention something if not applicable.

○ Is your product or service ready to go to market or is it still under development or being prototyped?

○ Did you invest in Research and Development? Over how long?

○ Have you completed market research?

○ Do you have any relevant patents?

○ Do you have any relevant trademarks?

○ What is the product lifecycle?

○ What is the market lifecycle?

○ Is any aspect of your product reliant on the intellectual property of a third party?

○ What aspects of your offering will foster repeat business?

1.4 Commercial Objectives

The reader is curious. You've made some attractive propositions so far, but where is the revenue going to come from? It's all well and good saying you're going to close 50 sales, but if this relies upon just one or two staff securing contracts in the first year with 30 government agencies then the investor is probably going to dismiss your concept as a pipe-dream.

It is a common mistake in business plans to fail to give adequate detail as to the exact commercial objectives. Plans appear loaded with 'fluff' and bold statements, whereas what is required are absolutes.

In the example business plan, two Directors have secured one contract and will work full-time to secure a further three contracts with Large Enterprise clients, and ten contracts within the SME sector. They will certainly be quizzed by investors as to whether those numbers are overly optimistic or, perhaps, whether they are too low.

Step by Step Guidance

○ You will find this section demands substantial review after you have completed your revenue forecast. It's part of the process.

○ Aim to answer the following questions: 'what revenues in what time frame?' and 'what activities in what time frame? For what benefit?'

○ If seeking funding, use a statement such as 'to raise £ x for the purpose of purchasing the required equipment', or whatever represents your actual scenario.

○ If applicable, offer detailed goals per revenue stream, such as from services, training, subscriptions, direct sales, indirect (channel) sales. Cite the percentage of total revenue each stream generates.

○ Use 'activity objectives' which relate to revenue goals, such as 'to increase the price of product 'x' in Q4'.

○ Highlight this section in yellow and double-check the final plan to ensure these numbers tally throughout your document.

1.5 Mission Statement

If you feel you must include a mission statement, and there is no obligation to do so, then you must avoid pithiness, rambling and clichés. Here is a truly appalling example emailed to me by a client asking for my thoughts. I think she found it online:

> *"Artists In Business" magazine is for the artist who is a worker at any level. The magazine has a commitment to be a platform to profile artists who are representing artistic vision in the marketplace and who can both encourage and provide role models to other men and women. Group Publishing, through its magazine, books, and editorial content, will be a vessel to inform artists about artistic principles in everyday business and will encourage interaction among artists as business people. Our mission is to promote the concept of "community" in the workplace."*

Why *'a worker at any level'*? Wouldn't *'worker'* suffice? Likewise, *'to other men and women'* … why not, simply, *'people'*? As to the second sentence, it leaves the reader breathless but none the wiser. In the sample business plan, I've offered an example to 'fill the gap' while hastening to add that I have never myself offered a mission statement:

> *'Facilitating business growth through captivating marketing content'*

To guide your thoughts further, consider these two outstanding examples:

> *'A simple, inexpensive vehicle affordable by all!'* – Henry Ford

> *'To solve unsolved problems innovatively'* – 3M Corporation

Step by Step Guidance

○ Keep it short and snappy: one sentence maximum.

○ Avoid fluff and hyperbole. Of course you want 'to be the leader in your field', why else would you be starting the business?

○ Ask someone else to create your mission statement, a third party might offer something resonating from a client's perspective.

○ No serious financier would deny investment as a result of you omitting this altogether, but trite clichés do turn people off.

1.6 Keys to Success

In addressing 'Keys to Success', your goal is to convey your appreciation that the business has specific challenges which must be met, but don't confuse this section with 'Risk Analysis'. That is addressed later.

Move your thinking beyond financial targets and instead focus on the management deliverables, such as what hurdles stand between success and failure? It is redundant to state that you must 'achieve targeted sales levels' etc. Surely you can conceive something more engaging?

Step by Step Guidance

There are unlimited possibilities as to what you might wish to include here, but examples of essential topics include the following as a minimum.

○ Is there a particular marketing goal which must be achieved? Why?

○ Is there particular capital equipment for which financing is fundamental? Are there various growth stages at which further capital investment is demanded?

○ Do you, your staff or your product require any specific qualifications, certifications or licenses in advance?

○ Does the business depend on certain third parties for approval, such as a reseller agreement from a software vendor, planning permission etc.?

○ Are there any product development milestones which must be completed over the course of the first three years?

1.7 Start-up Summary

You conclude the first section of your business plan with a snapshot of the finances required to get the project off the ground. This section will also be included in your 'five-page Executive Plan'.

The breakdown is to address exactly how much money must be raised, from what sources, and how will it be allocated? It also conveys the loan to investment ratio.

Expect an investor to interrogate you on this topic. It's to no one's benefit if you run out of cash early. This is also why one tends to plan for reserves not allocated for cash flow support.

Businesses with a solid trading history and seeking to expand are strongly advised to seek guidance from an accountant.

Step by Step Guidance

There are many potential formats for this table, and the example provided is geared very much towards the start-up:

○ Avoid excessive detail and be realistic. There's no advantage in low-balling the numbers and much to be said for inflating them by 25% to cover the inevitable surprises.

○ Your start-up expenses should detail the key categories of expense to be incurred before you commence operations. The topics which would always be expected include any costs for legal, accounting, premises, capital equipment, training, franchise fees and so forth. Encapsulate topics with 'Other purchases', and 'Other Expenditures' as required

○ Have a go, and if you are in the least bit uncomfortable with accounting basics, then seek guidance. Your prospective investor will probably know the format very well and it's essential that this section inspires trust.

Section Two: The Business

2.1 Company Summary

To provide the reader with a detailed overview of all legal aspects of the trading entity. If yours is an established business, you might have additional details depending upon your circumstances. If in doubt, include additional information.

Step by Step Guidance

At a minimum, you must include the details below:

O   Registered name exactly as listed at Companies House.

O   Trading name. Stipulate this even if it is the same as the registered name.

O   Registered address

O   Correspondence address (if different from registered address)

O   The type of business formation (Ltd., LLP, Partnership etc.)

O   Registrar

O   Registration number

- O Date of registration
- O Share capital
- O Telephone
- O Email
- O Website

2.2 Company Ownership

To provide a crystal clear review of who owns the company, including a summary of those who have maybe been issued shares but have no active role. There is nothing complex about this.

Step by Step Guidance

- O Create a simple table which lists the shareholders' name, position and share ownership.
- O Ensure the reader can see immediately if there are un-issued shares.

2.3 Management Summary

To offer a brief summary of who will be responsible for operations. In a larger business, this section might include senior employees, such as 'Lead Developer', or 'Head of Human Resources'.

Your task will be much easier if all Directors have a fully completed profiles on the LinkedIn business networking website. These should be thoroughly revised and updated, tailored as far as possible to emphasise suitability for launching a start-up or expanding an existing business. Stress credibility and capability.

Extend beyond the example as suits your business, but avoid the temptation to give too much detail.

Step by Step Guidance

- O Highlight the experience and investment of the Directors

○ Summarise each role and responsibility

○ Reference a single outstanding career achievement

○ Reference any Non-executive Director(s), Business Angel, or if there is an external Board of Directors.

2.4 Directors

Because the Management and the Directors might not be exactly the same, this section serves to offer condensed C.V.'s.

The inclusion of a 'Curious Fact' can make your team stand out as more rounded people and provide a gentle 'ice-breaker' when meeting with investors. You will know your plan has been thoroughly reviewed if this is brought up in conversation.

Save the long-winded curriculum vitae for the appendix and just stick to the absolute essentials for this recap of key staff credentials.

Step by Step Guidance

○ Experience: Cover the past ten years or so.

○ Education: Cite the most significant educational achievement.

○ Summary: Use just a few lines to pique interest. Highlight any notable career achievements.

○ Curious Fact: Entirely optional, but the one opportunity to convey the 'human' aspect of who you are.

2.5 Investors

In all likelihood, your business plan is also being used in an endeavour to raise capital. Equally your goal might be to entice another business partner to join your day to day operations. This section is your sales pitch: what do you want and why?

Except for the most remarkable business models, start-ups are advised to avoid detailing an exit plan. It suggests an unpleasant degree of arrogance and an 'I'm only it for the money' attitude. Better to reference the stage at which *'the business might reasonably be expected to attract buyers'*.

There are many potential permutations but, as with all parts, brevity is the key. Potential investors will have their own formulas, expectations or outright demands.

Step by Step Guidance

○ Open with a declaration of what you are seeking.

○ If you are seeking investment, then explain how that will be utilised to enhance your business objectives.

○ Lay out the basic detail of how you might propose to pay dividends.

○ If you believe the business might be ready to sell in three years, this is when to detail the exit plan.

2.6 Location and Facilities

Do you require business premises at the outset or is yours the sort of business which may be run from home-based offices? Starting a business with the most minimal overhead protects your cash flow and reduces stress.

For the majority of operations, premises are indeed essential, and if yours is a client centric operation then the costs scale proportionately. Investors don't see rent and utilities as an ROI, but they do want to see caution.

Unless you are offering a significant appendix, then a draft of the lease is not required, and then then only if it is of fundamental relevance, such as for a large retail operation. Similarly, if you believe a photograph of the premises is demanded, include one in this part of the business plan but then reference any others, along with floor plans and architect's conceptualisations in the appendices

Step by Step Guidance

○ If you can use a serviced office or, indeed, do without an office altogether this is worth highlighting. Offices equal overhead, an investor will not be displeased to see their cash gong on something other than rent, utilities and related additional costs.

○ Describe the facility and explain why it's suitable. Is there adequate parking for staff and clients?

○ You will require communications: do mobile telephones work there? Is there verified internet connectivity and of what type (fibre optic or copper wire)?

○ Describe the location in terms of road and public transportation connections, and detail the advantages.

○ Are there any relevant anchor businesses nearby?

○ If relevant, detail the demographics and local economics as may apply to your business.

○ Depending on your business will you require any special permits, licenses, fire safety, change of use permits or other?

○ What are the upgrade or refurbishment considerations and are the costs fully analysed? Such an analysis can be in the appendix.

○ Is the lease period suitable for your activity? What are the escape clauses? These terms must be explicit.

2.7 Professional Advisors

As an existing business, the credentials of your professional advisers can enhance your image, especially if they include well established firms. For a start-up, presenting a business plan which includes these details creates a significantly more favourable impression.

If you have not yet established an agreement with each of the above, do request permission to include these details in your business plan. Such permission is rarely withheld.

Step by Step Guidance

○ For your banker, accountant, legal adviser, include the business name, address, contact name, position, telephone number and website.

○ For your Non-executive Director(s), at this stage offer only their contact name and telephone number.

2.8 Recruitment of Key Employees

Naturally, as your business commences, you are likely to require people with particular trade or commercial skills. Key questions include determining when they need to be hired, how will you find them and how much they will cost?

Assumptions are dangerous, so be certain you have thoroughly researched availability and the market demands for compensation packages. Reference online salary and benefits checkers to gain insight, and remember to factor-in the full costs of employment.

Step by Step Guidance

○ Detail any role which is especially unusual, requires formal training, certifications or experience.

○ What is the total cost of the compensation package?

○ How will you find these key staff? Will you use an agency or seek out directly?

○ Do you have potential candidates?

○ Can outsourcing lower these overheads?

2.9 HR & Organisational Chart

The goal is to show at a glance who will report to who, and this highlights to investors that you have fully considered the implications: how can the Managing Director be selling effectively if he has eight direct reports, for example?

For sophisticated organisational charts there are several flexible packages available online, including some which are free to use.

Step by Step Guidance

○ If your enterprise has fewer than ten people, then include a full organisational chart, endeavouring to fit it into half a page.

○ For a more complex operation, consider if you can reduce much of the organisation chart down to 'roles'.

O Beware of tiny graphics! Incorporate an A3 sized full fold-out chart either here or inserted into the appendix.

Section Three: Market Overview

3.1 Market Overview

It is most likely that a potential investor is unfamiliar with your industry niche, and possibly even the entire industry. In previous sections you have compiled your business case, but now you need to prove you've done your homework.

The market overview is entirely 'top level'. Is this industry stable and mature, or only in its infancy? What of technological improvements in recent years and how have they challenged the status quo? Is the market concentrated among a few key players or highly fragmented?

For example, if you are entering the publishing industry then you might highlight how e-Books were thought to signal the death knell of print publishers, and yet many print publishers are now enjoying outstanding success. Likewise, technology has introduced 'print on demand', which has eliminated the need for small titles to be held as stock and, perhaps later, destined for pulp. This would develop into a summary indicating, perhaps, that publishing is leaner than before but very much alive and well.

Manufacturers, importers, retailers and even software publishers within traditional niches are able to quantify clearly their anticipated competition. This is true also for the services industry. It's far harder for the business selling a particular knowledge expertise to market, but effort must be invested in evaluating those whom you will be challenging.

You must endeavour to be balanced, and to convey your thoughts as if to someone who is educated but unfamiliar with the specifics of your industry.

Given the variability of possibilities, the framework below should steer you on the right path.

Step by Step Guidance

○ Define your marketplace and any submarket. Note if there is a further overlap to any other industry, in the same way that Starbucks© is a coffee shop franchise which also sells food.

○ Examine the age of the market, the number of vendors and their longevity. Is the industry undergoing growth or decline?

○ What aspect of the industry demonstrates there is growth and room for a new entrant?

○ Examine the market from the client's point of view. What do they want? Why? What are the obstacles and what has prevented the incumbent providers from satisfying this demand?

○ Why will clients want your service? Are you bringing something new from the outside or are you a disruptive force with a vision as to how you can create new markets while also capturing existing market share.

○ A summary. It might be the only point the reader of your business plan bother with, so make it stand out.

3.2 Market Trends

What are the buzzwords of the industry now? What is the big news?

Step by Step Guide

○ Is there consolidation of vendors in your market? Are they merging or are some just failing? If failing, why? Conversely, describe how new entrants are performing, and what lessons can be learned.

○ If you would describe your market as having various tiers of vendors, what are the differentiators between how the various tiers are performing? Why?

○ Has the market shown local, regional or national acceptance for a new entrant to the market? Explain.

○ Will your entrance create new customers or will you just compete for a slice of the existing market share? How? Why? Can this be changed?

3.3 Demographic, Economic, Cultural, Social Factors

The consideration of demographic, economic and cultural factors is one which can be an essential part of a business plan, such as opening a restaurant. Conversely, in Business to Business (B2B) sales, it is often the case that only minor acknowledgement is required, and then largely with respect to macro-economics.

Step by Step Guide

○ Demographics factors you might have to consider include the median ages and socio-economic status of your target market, and where they are geographically in relation to your business. How will you reach them? How does this affect your marketing? Use statistics.

○ In Business to Business (B2B) sales, it is fair to say that demographics generally play a far lesser role but some industries are certainly more biased towards one gender than others. Explain sensitively if you see any advantages for your business with respect to the demographics.

○ Economic factors for the restaurateur are significant. These will relate to the macro-economic, such as ascertaining the disposable income in your target market, the local average spent on a meal, the preference for particular types of beverage and more. Broader economic factors will include inflation or shortages of critical goods. For example, if you were about to open a coffee shop, you would want to cite (and reference) any report that forecasts coffee prices are to remain steady or fall over the coming three years.

○ Macro-economic factors for B2B might include referencing employment trends. Broad economic factors might reference the cost of raw materials and how these could rise or fall depending on the costs of oil.

○ Cultural considerations for the restaurateur might highlight the growing demand for food of a particular ethnic origin. Why? By people of that ethnicity or from a different one? What data do you have which supports the existence of your target market and their willingness to buy?

O Cultural considerations in B2B are less obvious and often not relevant at all. There are exceptions though: for example, non-French people, no matter how proficient they are in the language, can struggle to sell in France. Is your target market in France and how are you impacted?

3.4 The Market Segment

As with the topic of demographics, the content for detailing your market segment differs entirely according to your industry and whether you will operate in business to business, retail, services, manufacturing and so forth.

While the guide below should steer you in the right direction, the example in the sample business plan is typical as might be used by a niche vendor in the business to business arena.

Step by Step Guide

O Exactly which aspect of the market are you targeting? Is there a profile of 'competitor' which you need to clarify as not truly in your niche?

O Outline who will buy your product and why? Include any market surveys or other supporting data if available.

O Can you define the size of the market and what percentage you hope to capture from the competition?

O Within your precise niche, how do you intend to develop your products or services over time?

O What attributes of your business suggest potential for longevity?

3.5 Products & Services

Your reader has been waiting for this. Remember, though, this is not a sales brochure, so stick to simple language and explain what each of your core products or services do, and why they do it so well.

If you have brochures already prepared, give them a prominent reference and insert them into the appendix.

Some products are too complex for the layman. Consider if a technology White Paper could be of service? This also should be offered in the appendix. Either way, you are going to have to explain the technology simply and clearly.

Few things gain the interest of a savvy investor more than keywords such as 'subscription', 'Professional Services', 'rental' and the like. These are seen as 'money for old rope', the easy revenue generators so often overlooked.

The final point is to close with a list of potential developments for the coming years.

Step by Step Guide

O Detail each of your core products, or product lines, offering a short description of each.

O If at all relevant, detail any ancillary services you offer such as:

     i)   Consultancy

     ii) Training

     iii) Post-sales support

     iv) Product upgrades

     v) Rentals

     vi) Subscription services

     vii) Memberships

O Close by offering a list of other products and services which you envision being able to bring to the market in the future.

3.6 Risk Factors & Implications

There are 'Risk Factors' for every business. Technological risk factors include such aspects of business as the success of alternative technology which renders your key product offering less desirable or even obsolete. Consider also the implications if a key component or equipment upon which you rely was to become unavailable or unserviceable.

A risk factor which is often overlooked is emerging technology entering the market which offers your competition sudden, massive, cost savings. You might well be aware of this technology but recognise that the investment is far beyond your budget. How will you respond?

Commercial risk factors are more numerous. There might be a market rejection of your new product or service, now or in the near future. What of government legislation? Is there any risk that your business model is threatened by pending legislation or even movement in that direction? Researching your industry for all potential trends is of paramount importance. Consider also risks which might be posed by weather, climate, changing social tastes, taxation, tariffs,

Do not state that 'there are no risk factors'! If your business is truly successful, then it is sure to be emulated.

Step by Step Guidance

- Describe the technological risks? How severe? What strategy is in in place to mitigate them?

- Describe the commercial risks? How severe? What strategy is in in place to mitigate them?

- Describe the environmental risks? How severe? What strategy is in in place to mitigate them?

- List the key business attributes which offer risk mitigation.

- Close with a statement which summarises the fundamental strategy which insulates your business from the primary risks identified above.

3.7 S.W.O.T. Analysis

Prepare a S.W.O.T Analysis in a table form as per the example in the sample business plan.

Step by Step Guidance

Be very frank with your assessment. You will need to justify your findings to any investor, and they also are likely to have done their research.

STRENGTHS

These are the tangible and intangible attributes of your business. They may relate to your people or your product. Above all, they are internal and within the ability of your organisation to control.

WEAKNESSES

Factors about your business which are threats to the business goals and objectives. What might be improved to diminish these weaknesses.

OPPORTUNITIES

Positive external factors which represent the reason for the business to be created, especially commercial market gaps. May include business, environment, people, places and timing

THREATS

These are strictly external factors over which the organisation has no control. Examples might include broad or macro-economic factors, a competitor replicating your product, or indeed any factor which could harm your business and interfere with the achievement of your goals.

Section Four: Competition

4.1 Competitive Overview

The competitive overview demands a high degree of objectivity. It can be difficult to offered absolute statistics, but offering evidence of your research is important. Remember, this is a business plan and not a thesis.

Step by Step Guidance

○ Summarise the tiers within the targeted market segment. Offer a profile of the top competitors in each.

○ In which tier or tiers will you be competing, and why?

○ Explore the tiers further and explain why your business will focus on just one or multiple tiers.

○ Summarise the competition in your target tier(s). How many and what characteristics or trends do they share? How long trading?

○ In more depth, what is the quality of the competition. Are they growing, profitable, successful, failing? Have you reviewed their annual reports or general finances?

○ Summarise the above and explain why there is room for a new market entrant.

4.2 Competitors and Type of Competition

Depending on your industry, market segment, and overall competition you may need to expand upon this section but very often only the briefest summary is required.

Step by Step Guidance

○ At a minimum, provide the full name of each competitor in a table form, and detail if they are a direct or indirect competitor.

○ An investor will want to review the competition too, so include the website URL's.

○ Expanding upon the above, consider a paragraph on each noting reputation, innovation, financial advantages and disadvantages, focus, and other factors which relate to how your business might successfully challenge them or, as applicable, merely co-exist.

4.3 Competitors Strengths & Weaknesses

Research is key to success, and nothing evidences your research so effectively as a thorough and well-presented table of competitive strengths and weaknesses. Remember, though, this is not a thesis so reference your appendix if there is detailed analysis supporting your findings. The table which results may fill an entire page.

Step by Step Guidance

○ Create a table which lists your competitors. Place your business as the final entry (whether at the bottom or extreme right, depending on the format).

○ Select a minimum of five measurable criteria. There are no hard and fast rules, but a price comparison is one of the universal elements.

○ The balance of the criteria could be very specific to your market segment or they might be much more subjective, opinion-driven elements such as flavour, imagination and so forth.

○ Additional criteria which might be used include: USP, location, speed of delivery, product range, marketing, brand awareness etc. You have to decide what is relevant for your business.

4.4 Competitive Advantage

You have compared your business against the competition in a tabular form, so now summarise the table with a narrative. Keep it 'punchy' by using affirmative, positive statements: this is no time to be overly modest, but it must remain professional and lacking in clichés.

Step by Step Guidance

○ Introduce with an affirmative statement as to your advantage.

○ Outline first advantage and the benefit to the client base.

○ Outline the second advantage and the benefit to the client base.

○ Offer a positive conclusion. Summarise your competitive advantages in terms of creating both positive cash flow and profitability.

Section Five: Sales & Marketing

5.1 Sales & Marketing Objectives

In all likelihood, your sales and marketing plan is as long as your business plan. The investor doesn't need this, they need a simple summary and, as such, one page is ample.

Step by Step Guidance

○ State that you have a Sales and Marketing Plan available for review. Ensure it is complete.

○ Define your initial marketing objective. This could be as simple as ensuring that potential clients know you exist or ensuring that you can be found by internet search engines. Define some criteria for success, such as 'to appear in the top five Google search results'.

○ Define your secondary marketing objective. This might be a summary of your brand and product positioning. How will this be achieved?

○ State your sales objectives. Specifically, identify sources of revenue, sales cycles, volumes, and from what customers. Express this in terms of percentages of total revenue.

○ Define the criteria for ensuring you can fulfil your sales objectives. Such criteria might range from achieving a minimum level of sales presentations, product demonstrations, footfall, table covers or services rendered. Are you establishing criteria for measuring additional sales, for example the sale of support and maintenance contracts?

5.2 Financial Objectives of the Sales & Marketing

In (5.1) above, we painted a broad picture, and now we offer specifics. The objective now is to summarise exact, measurable, criteria.

Step by Step Guidance

○ Restate the annual revenue and EBIT targets.

○ Summarise the volume of sales to achieve FY1 targets. Offer a simple breakdown of revenue by product, vertical or whatever criteria fits your business.

○ Note pending business such as assured contracts, provisional bookings, or other assurances of early commitment to purchase. This can be especially challenging in some sectors (retail, catering, insurance etc.), but for a manufacturer or service industry venture it is entirely reasonable.

○ Are there any other criteria which enhance your likelihood of achieving your financial objectives? This could range from statistical expectation of selling a certain percentage of service contracts to a catering operation noting a forthcoming trade conference. It would be an unusual business for which no enhancements can be found.

5.3 Target Markets

Whether this is titled 'Target Market', 'Route to Market' or similar, the reader wants to see exactly who you will be targeting. Keep it brief and offer justifications.

Step by Step Guidance

O State clearly your general business model: B2B, retail, e-Commerce or whatever combination of the above. If B2B, will you be selling directly, via a resellers or distributors, or a combination?

O Define the size of the marketplace by whatever criteria might apply.

O Is there a 'typical' customer profile? This might include parameters such as age, sex, income, lifestyle.

O Identify any criteria on which your marketing focus will concentrate. Why?

5.4 Positioning the Brand

Brand positioning matters as much for the discount retailer as it does for a prestige vehicle dealership. Clients react to brands, and the way they are presented, in strange ways. They might dismiss a brand as too expensive because of the image. Conversely, in some sectors, customers may avoid a brand deemed not expensive enough. In the UK one can compare Lidl and Waitrose supermarkets and see the effect.

For the majority of businesses, this section may be particularly brief.

Step by Step Guidance

O Is the product or service a 'must have', or merely a 'desirable'?

O How critical is the price point, or is quality more important?

O To what extent does after sales service affect your brand?

O Does your business establish a client relationship? Is this product or service based?

O Are there other factors which co-exist, such as a reputation for quality or specialisation?

5.5 Pricing

To reiterate, the investor probably does not know too much about your niche, let alone your industry. Excessive detail here is superfluous, so paint a broad picture.

No matter what, the investor should see at a glance that you average product falls into a general price band. Is your 'typical' sale going to be £1,000 or £50,000?

Step by Step Guidance

○ Introduce with a clear statement about your price positioning relative to your competition. Is it low, medium, high or premium? Justify why this is the correct strategy.

○ Do not list all of your products. Such detail is irrelevant. Offer critical highlights and explain how the price compares to similar products or services within your market segment.

○ Offer supplementary information to explain to the reader what the client might receive in addition to the core product. This is your own 'value add'.

5.6 Product Marketing & Promotion

For your product or services, offer an overview of such elements as the quality, branding, packaging or servicing. Define how the product is introduced to potential clients, and by what media or actions.

Step by Step Guide

○ State your quality proposition. What is it about your business which differentiates you from your competition? Try to offer specifics.

○ State your value proposition. You might not be the cheapest but what is it that you offer which will save the client time, money, reputation, inconvenience etc.?

○ How will the above be promoted? Naturally an internet presence is a part but what exactly? What other outreach strategies will be utilised? These can range from 'open days' and seminars, to various forms of media advertising, product trials, free software applications – the possibilities are endless but all should exist in your draft marketing plan.

5.7 Service

For your product or services, can you define what service your business will offer clients in the event of difficulty? This might cover disputes over product delivery timeframes and range to a customer feeling generally dissatisfied with the product. For different businesses, the approaches can vary significantly.

Step by Step Guide

○ Is there a service level agreement? Describe any particular features which differentiate your approach? How might this work to your competitive advantage?

○ Is there a quality control policy? Describe any particular features which differentiate your approach? How might this work to your competitive advantage?

○ Is there a returns policy? Describe any particular features which differentiate your approach? How might this work to your competitive advantage?

○ Is there an industry or government oversight body such as an Ombudsman? Explain how this operates to the advantage of the business.

5.9 Distribution Channels

For some businesses the distribution channels can be of extreme importance and complexity, and this is often the case for software vendors. The investor is looking for a broad picture, so expand this section only if the channel itself has a particular bearing upon revenues. For example, if training your reseller channel represents a significant income or expenditure, then add more detail.

Step by Step Guide

○ Reiterate your sales model: are selling directly or indirectly? To the public, businesses or to both?

O For your indirect sales, will you sell to wholesalers, use a reseller channel, work through retailers, or a combination?

O What other routes to market will you incorporate? Examples include manual orders through the internet, e-Commerce, mail order, telesales, your own retail premises, face to face, via software application or other?

O Define any key criteria for your channel. For example, if retail, then how many staff are required and what levels of training are required? Through resellers, is there a requisite training or certification process?

5.10 Key Suppliers

For some businesses, the supplier relationship is paramount. Perhaps your business requires approval, training, certification? Are there fees to be paid to secure the trading relationship?

Step by Step Guidance

O List suppliers by name and function. Have you secured payment terms? Detail them. What credit limits are established?

O Are any relevant volume discounts offered?

O Are there any discounts for early payment?

O Are there other considerations such as quarterly rebates?

5.11 Customers

There are few things more pleasing to the eye of an investor, especially when reviewing start-up's, than to see a list of 'deals in the bag'. Indeed, every effort must be invested to securing either a contract in principal – or even more – or at the very least some form of market analysis which indicates clients who indicate support.

Step by Step Guidance

O Identify the client (with their permission), or anonymise the name.

○ Detail the contract value.

○ Describe the client.

○ Insert a quotation.

○ Profile the client.

○ Reveal your sales 'pipeline': other projects which are in development.

Section Six: Operations

6.1 Operating Plan

Few aspects of the business plan are as complex to as the Operating Plan. The temptation for many is to offer far too much detail when all that is really required within the context of a business plan is a six-point summary of: facilities, staff, suppliers, inventory, equipment and process.

The guidance notes give individual coverage for the knowledge worker, services and retailers, and manufacturers.

Step by Step Guidance

FOR THE KNOWLEDGE WORKER

Strictly speaking, 'Knowledge Workers' fall within the category of being a Service Industry, and yet this niche includes such disciplines as consultants, lawyers, and many other professional and creative fields. They are differentiated entirely from other services insofar as they share little in common with hotels or automotive repair facilities: after all, the lawyer needs little more than a telephone, computer and access to a law library. When preparing the Operating Plan, the Knowledge Worker has the easiest task. The investor doesn't require huge detail: encapsulate and abbreviate.

○ Facilities. Provide an overview of the required office infrastructure, noting ease of access, importance of location, capacity for expansion and other key attributes.

○ Staffing. Indicate the total number of staff and reference any specialist roles for which exacting experience, training or formal qualifications are demanded. Are the staff available?

○ Suppliers: Are there particular specialist suppliers required, such as access to knowledge-centric databases, physical publications, or core materials for the creative worker?

○ Inventory. While uncommon for the knowledge worker, in the example business plan it may be seen that a core body of work is intended to be produced ahead of commencing operations. There is an implicit cost, even if one might ascribe that to marketing.

○ Equipment. Specialist IT systems and computer hardware might need to be specified and installed. Are there any special considerations?

○ Process. What is being produced and are there any special considerations? Can you differentiate your service? Will there be areas of particular expertise? How can these be translated into competitive advantages?

FOR SERVICES, RETAILERS AND MANUFACTURERS

Traditional businesses tend to have intensive demands for both staffing and physical infrastructure. The investor expects to see high-level assessments of how the management will deliver the service, and that key topics such as infrastructure and inventory are thoroughly researched.

○ Facilities. Summarise the facilities and the hurdles in preparing them for operations, including topics such as surveys, architects, interior designers, contractors, health and safety.

○ Staffing. Indicate the total number of staff and reference any specialist roles for which exacting experience, training or formal qualifications are demanded. Are the staff available?

○ Suppliers: The supply chain is of extreme importance, so explain critical areas and – especially – reference the availability of alternatives. Are you reliant upon one source or brand? Can the risk be diminished?

○ Inventory. Inventory is cash, and cash belongs in the bank, so how much inventory will you hold in terms of value and period? What is your reasoning?

○ Equipment. Demands for specialist equipment can upset many business plans. Is the equipment readily available? Have you properly analysed the delivery, installation, configuration and training implications? What of service and support for critical components?

○ Process. How will the service be delivered? What are the key attributes to ensure it is satisfactory? Is there anything which might be explained to differentiate your service? What aspects can be translated into competitive advantages?

6.2 Overview [Technical or Process?]

The knowledge worker will create a simple technical summary of the deliverable, while other businesses will need to be more expansive, generally focussing on the process.

The retailer will explain such aspects as how the facility creates a particular customer experience, or how product placements will be utilised to best effect. What of the customer engagement process? Is there a particular POS and inventory control program which will minimise freight costs and automate inventory management?

The manufacturer will detail the production cycle and highlight the advantages of the capital equipment selected. This latter point is particularly important as capital expenditure is disliked by most investors since any failure of the business renders such equipment almost valueless. Stress the competitive advantages such capital equipment creates.

The investor probably doesn't want to know how to build a house or to program a computer – or whatever it is that you do – but there is a demand to see that you know how to do it. If your process is too technical, move the required detail into the appendix and offer a highlight here. Stick to one page, or two at the most. Only for the most extremely technical proposals might three pages be required.

Step by Step Guidance

○ Write a brief summary of the technology or service from a product perspective. Don't repeat what has already been explained but give precise details.

○ Write a 'process walk-through', from receipt of purchase order to despatching the deliverable. The hotel operator will detail the planned customer experience, while the manufacturer will describe the conversion of raw materials into a tangible finished product.

○ Conclude with a synopsis of the 'systems' in place to drive success, quality, competitive advantage, security, safety, and client satisfaction.

6.3 Government Regulation

Summarise any relevant government regulation which apply to your business or industry in particular. If there are none, then state that accordingly.

Step by Step Guidance

○ Are any professional licenses or required?

○ Are there any restrictions related to the export of your product?

○ Does your product demand specific ISO or CE approvals?

○ Are you obliged to carry special insurance coverages?

○ Are you obliged to be a member of a particular trade organisation?

6.4 Equipment, Technology, R&D

Summarise any planned investment in equipment, technology or research and development. If there is none, then state that accordingly.

Step by Step Guidance

○ For each category, describe the nature of the investment, when it will commence, why it is required, and how much it will cost.

○ Detail the 'trigger' which will prompt the expenditure.

○ Explain the benefit to the business in terms of how it will reduce costs, increase sales etc.

6.5 Environmental Considerations

Summarise any relevant environmental considerations which apply to your business or industry in particular. If there are none, then state that accordingly.

Step by Step Guidance

○ Can you be classed as 'green', 'eco-friendly' or similar? This can be a huge positive for your branding.

○ Are there any steps you can take to reduce emissions or wastage? This can be as simple as not printing paper, relying on solar power or heat exchangers for a percentage of your energy requirements.

6.6 Action Plan & Timetable

The Action Plan is presented as a Gantt Chart, and may be as simple as in the example business plan or fill an entire page. The objective is to present the major milestones and timeframes for fulfilment both prior to opening the business and covering the first weeks of operations.

For all but the simplest businesses, a Gantt chart is an absolute planning requirement. There is no need to offer the investor every tiny detail – save that for your office wall – so just cover the key points. For example, when must the lease be signed in order that the facilities may be prepared for use?

It must be legible. Consider an A3 sized fold-out within your business plan.

Step by Step Guidance

○ Typical sub-headings include: management, facilities, capital purchases, training, staffing, inventory, marketing, and sales.

○ Under each sub-heading identify key accomplishments required. Remember to allow for delays: if your trademark is important, be aware that approval can take anywhere from three weeks to six months.

Section Seven: Financials

7.1 FY1 Cash Flow: Revenue & Expense Forecast

The first financial report to produce is the Revenue and Expense forecast for the first twelve months of operations. This is also referred to as an Income Statement.

Step by Step Guidance

○ Detail your key sources of revenue using broad categories where appropriate. Only rarely will more than eight categories be required. The parameters used might detail exact products or by product category (such as software, hardware, professional services, etc.). As in the sample plan it might be a combination of the two.

○ Enter the anticipated revenue per month for each category. Start with your most pessimistic projections. Calculate the total revenue per month.

○ Detail your key classes of expenditure using broad categories where appropriate. There are no absolute rules, but certainly rent, wages, Director's drawings, utilities and so forth are expected. Add more if required but don't include irrelevant entries such as 'miscellaneous' and 'other'.

○ Enter realistic expectations for all classes of expenditure. As far as possible use researched numbers. Remember to add 30% to staff salaries to cover benefits and employer overheads. Calculate the total expenditure per month.

○ Subtract the expenses from the revenue to produce your gross profit or loss each month before taxes.

○ Analyse the year as a whole by subtracting total expense from total revenue. If the result is a negative, then you might have a problem: can you justify increasing your sales projections?

○ Many businesses do not make a profit for three years, but if one is seeking investment then consider every option: what can be done to achieve break-even or better in the first year? Your first year projections will normally indicate a loss, but as long as the total loss doesn't exceed 50% of your cash reserves, then it is not cause for alarm. Above that level indicates that you might need further investment.

○ Refine and revise. Repeat until you believe every value entered is achievable or realistic.

7.2 FY1-3 Cash Flow: Revenue & Expense Forecast

In the United Kingdom we expect to see a three-year revenue and expense forecast, while in the United States the norm is to detail a five-year plan.

The process is the same for FY1, except that once completed for all 36 or 60 months, it is consolidated down to Quarters.

Step by Step Guidance

○ No matter the profit or loss for FY1, an investor expects to see substantial progress in FY2 and FY3.

○ Your business plan should incorporate minimum growth of >30% per annum. Aiming for less raises alarm bells for any investor.

○ It is not necessarily unrealistic to see 100% growth rates for the first three years, but thereafter growth tends to slow significantly, rarely exceeding 40%.

○ Beware of the 'hockey stick', that is a projection which doesn't offer steady growth but a sudden skyward projection. Ideally, one should be able to place a ruler along the growth chart and see only minor variations. If it is otherwise, then be prepared to offer substantial and authoritative justification.

7.3 Cash Flow Forecast (Graphics)

Insert a graph (line chart) which details cash flow by month for FY1

Insert a graph (line chart) which details cash flow by quarter for FY1 – FY3

7.4 Source of Revenue (Graphics)

Insert a graph (pie chart) which details the source of revenue per month for FY1

Insert a graph (pie chart) which details the source of revenue per quarter for FY1 – FY3

Part Three
Model Business Plan

Business Plan for

Market Précis Ltd. ™

Revision 3.5 Dated 2 February 2017

Directors   Jack Hamilton

Lucy Brown

Market Précis Limited

Suite 1, 1 Mayfair, London, W1A 1AW, United Kingdom

A limited liability company registered in England & Wales, Reg. No. 1010101

Telephone +44(0)1202 000 1111 | Email management@marketprecis.com

www.marketprecis.com

Facilitating business growth through captivating marketing content

Table of Contents

Market Précis Ltd. ™

SECTION ONE: Introduction

1.1 EXECUTIVE SUMMARY

Market Précis is a newly formed Content Creation agency for the internet: we design, create and distribute innovative textual content for web-based marketing, particularly articles and blog pieces. In addition, we have designed in-house our own advanced digital marketing techniques and data analytics solutions.

Our target market is any SME with more than 50 staff, especially those operating in specific vertical industries. Our solutions fulfil the urgent demand for these businesses to add 'content' to their websites in order that they can achieve critical traffic and search engine page rankings. Client acquisition, especially for e-Commerce vendors, has become a significant overhead, and our value proposition is clear: we reduce this overhead by 40%.

This marketplace is relatively immature and in the United Kingdom there are only three established competitors. Following twelve months of R&D, we have secured two provisional contracts: one SME and one Large Enterprise.

Our Tiered Subscription model brings innovation to the sector. We offer Content as a Service (CaaS) which involves the rental of our data in the same manner that software is delivered. Our business model concentrates on the service itself, with contract renewal rates of at least 50%. This supports our year-on-year growth projections while offsetting demands for aggressive rates of new-client acquisition. Clients pre-pay for services, enabling us to operate with minimal debt at all times.

Based on an initial start-up investment of £120,000, Market Précis forecast FY1 revenues of £300,000 with an EBIT of £30,000. By FY3 this will increase to £775,000 revenue with an EBIT of £350,000.

In terms of cash generation, by the close of FY3 we will have achieved surplus cash (before taxes and dividends) of £430,000. Based upon a start-up investment of £120,000 this gives an ROI of 300%.

The operational plan relies on Business Process Outsourcing (BPO) services. This negates all significant capital expenditure requirements and eliminates staffing overheads.

Market Précis Ltd.™

The management consists of two Directors who are equal shareholders. Bringing considerable industry experience, they committed to funding £80,000 of the start-up costs and are seeking a further £40,000 of investment.

The Directors of Market Précis invite additional active business partners, or investors who recognise the potential rewards and significant tax advantages of the well researched venture. Market Précis is approved by HMRC as a SEIS qualifying investment.

1.2   Business Overview

Market Précis is a specialist marketing support agency. We create original and innovative textual content for internet marketing, partnering directly with businesses of all sizes to ensure effective client acquisition campaigns.

Primarily, our content consists of professional articles and blog pieces, ranging from 500 – 2,500 words. These are combined with graphics, adjusted for Search Engine Optimisation and then broadcast. Typically, a client producing in-house will spend >£50,000 per year but with Business Précis this overhead is reduced by 40%.

> " Traditional creation. Innovative delivery. Monetisation. Application of leading-edge technology.

Demand is driven further by the fast-evolving nature of e-commerce, of which the United Kingdom is the most vigorous adopter. Given the profile of an e-Commerce buyer, not being found online equates to not just one lost sale but, potentially, to all future sales cycles. Our clients achieve more than savings: their own client acquisition rates grow by up to 40% and client retention is increased up to 70%.

We use our own contract network of professional authors for the creation, and we complete all back-office functions through our favoured Business Process Outsourcing (BPO) partner in Europe. This combination enables us to scale operations exactly according to client demand while eliminating all typical business contractual overheads. The business model is lean.

SUMMARY OF BUSINESS FEATURES

- o   Our solution is delivered through a tiered subscription model
- o   We offer a range of professional services (translation, graphics etc.)
- o   Specialisation in 4 specific vertical markets: Legal, Travel, Health, Lifestyle.
- o   All revenue is pre-paid
- o   Minimal capital expenditure is combined with exceptionally low overhead

The Directors are highly experienced, 'risk averse', industry professionals who have used their own assets to fund the business start-up. A considerable margin of safety is secured via a 7:1 ratio of funding vs. cash flow requirements during the first year.

1.3 Summary of Products and Services

Our products are fully developed, and ready to 'go to market'. We have invested almost a full year in market research, R&D, and product testing to validate our business plan.

Our core product is called MPContent which is a subscription based service for unique content required by corporate marketing departments. For an SME, this will include 72 articles and 96 blog pieces over the term of the service contract. For a Large Enterprise client these figures are doubled.

The use of annual subscriptions enables us to become integrated into the clients' business processes. The close relationship forms a partnership which counters the 'one time' product sale.

As shall be detailed below, this is a new product suite being introduced to a fast-growing niche within the internet-based marketing sector.

1.4 Commercial Objectives FY1

DEVELOP COMMERCIAL CONTRACT REVENUE FROM OUR CORE PRODUCT

- o Secure 4 subscription contracts for MPContent in the Large Enterprise sector, representing 30% of our revenue target.
- o Secure 12 subscription contracts for MPContent in the SME sector, representing 39% of our revenue target.
- o Achieve the remaining 31% of our revenue goals by selling our 2nd tier products and services to the initial MPContent clients.

DEVELOP TRAFFIC AND SUBSCRIPTION REVENUE

- o Leverage our MPWeb product to achieve > 120,000 unique visits per month for a total annual traffic count of 480,000 visits across our four portals. The goal: 96,000 subscribers of which 2,400 paying for 'Premium Content' access.

o Develop a reseller model with particular emphasis on offering our solution in other European countries.

1.5 Mission Statement

'Facilitating business growth through captivating marketing content'

1.6 Keys to Success

The keys to success for the for the first year of Business Précis operations include:

o Timely creation of the core content required to support our vertical markets.

o Ensuring the corporate website and is maximising engagement with the readership, and that it is streamlined with our social media marketing.

o Control of costs while securing initial contracts.

o Successful promotion our unique Landing Page technology through the leading search engines, with absolute emphasis upon Google. Our detailed marketing plan stipulates the metrics demanded.

o Execution of our own SEO strategy to build general readership, subscriptions and premium content subscriptions, thus achieving sales targets for affiliate advertising sales revenues.

o Future growth demands renewals of the subscription service, thus constant evaluation of client satisfaction levels is critical. This requires early completion of our post-sales benchmarking utility.

1.7 Start-up Summary

The start-up summary offers sufficient capital to be reasonably assured of achieving all required preparations, including advanced client acquisition.

The size of the investment is important to ensure that production can be scaled up according to market demand.

Market Précis Ltd.™

Start Up Expenses

Legal (incl. trademark)	£3,000
Accounting	£1,000
Insurance	£500
IT (Hardware / Network / Software))	£6,000
Marketing	£9,000
Pre-sales (3 months travel expense)	£9,000
Training	£4,000
Website design	£3,500
Freelance Agent Recruitment and validation	£4,000
Total Start-up Expenses	£40,000

Start-up Assets

Cash Required	£80,000
Long Term Assets	£0
Other Assets	£0
Total Start-up Assets	£80,000

Start-up Funding

Start-up Expenses	£40,000
Start-up Assets	£80,000
Total Start-up Funding Required	£120,000

Assets

Non-cash Assets from Start-up	£0
Cash Requirements from Start-up	£0
Additional Cash Raised	£0
Cash Balance on Starting Date	£80,000
Total Assets	£80,000

Liabilities

Liabilities	£0
Current Borrowing	£0
Long Term Liabilities	£0
Accounts Payable	£0
Other Current Liabilities	£0
Total Liabilities	£0

Capital

Co-owner 1	£40,000
Co-owner 2	£40,000
Co-owner 3	£40,000
Additional Investment Requirements	£0
Total Planed Investment	£120,000

146

Summary

Loss at Start-up	(£40,000)
Total Capital	£120,000
Total Liabilities	£0
Total Funding	**£80,000**

Market Précis Ltd.™

Section Two: The Business

2.1 Company Summary

Registered Name	Market Précis Limited
Trading as	Market Précis Limited
Registered Address	Suite 555, 111 Mayfair Avenue, London, W1A 1AW, United Kingdom
Type of Company	Limited Liability Company
Registered	Companies House, England & Wales,
Registration No.	1010101
Date of Registration	15 July 2016
Share Capital	£6,000
Telephone	+44(0)1202 111 2222
Email	management@marketprecis.com
Website	www.marketprecis.com

2.2 Company Ownership

Position	Name	Share Ownership
Director	Jack Hamilton	2,000
Director	Lucy Brown	2,000
Investor		0
Total Shares Issued		4,000
Shares not Issued		2,000

2.3 Management Summary

The founding Directors have each committed substantial personal investment, and they will be working together full time drive business growth. The team possess considerable industry-specific experience with highly complementary skill sets. Learn more by reviewing their LinkedIn profiles online.

Jack Hamilton carries the lead sales role, and will oversee all 'back office' functions, including accounting.

Lucy Brown will work in partnership with Jack Hamilton to develop sales. She will oversee the outsourced customer service and contract renewal staff.

The team shall be advised by Dr. Abdul Doolittle, the respected financier and Business Angel. Dr. Doolittle has been appointed to the role of Non-Executive Director. His expert guidance and oversight in launching 'high tech' SME's is invaluable.

2.4 Directors

JACK HAMILTON MANAGING DIRECTOR

Experience   2005 – 2015, Sales & Marketing Director, XYX Plc., London

1998 – 2005, Marketing Director, ABC Ltd., London

Education   BSc (Hons) Accountancy, University of Durham

Summary   30 years of experience in developing IT businesses from start-up. An expert at implementing successful sales and marketing solutions in the computer industry. He has taken one business from start-up to a listing on the London Stock Exchange. Jack brings expertise of outsourcing solutions.

He is a prolific author on business topics, and has been published in many major international publications.

Curious Fact   Jack plays concert grade piano in his spare time.

Market Précis Ltd.™

LUCY BROWN	SALES DIRECTOR
Experience	2010 – 2015, Sales Director, XYX Plc., London
	2000 – 2010, Senior Sales Executive, AAA Ltd., London
Education	BA Business Studies, University of Nottingham

Summary   A marketing industry expert, Lucy specialises in global 'C' Level sales across multiple verticals. She headed the sales team of XYZ Plc. to an average growth rate of 32% for three consecutive years.

Curious Fact   Lucy climbed Mount Everest while still attending University

2.5   Investors

The Directors of Market Précis welcome expressions of interest from investors.

We propose a share dividend option, based upon a quarterly distribution of 30% of retained cash following three successive profitable quarters. This will be conditional upon achievement of 70% of our sales targets averaged over the six months preceding.

Any additional early-stage investment will be directed to securing market share, and also towards increasing our web-portal presence which has the potential to be a strong revenue generator.

2.6   Location and Facilities

The Directors do not foresee and requirement to lease offices in the first year of trading since all technical operations are to be outsourced to Eastern Europe, leaving the UK as a pure sales operation. Clients who wish to see our operations centre can fly from most major UK airports.

There is the option in FY2 to take a serviced office if required. If so, it would be a contract only for 'access on demand' to satisfy both client and internal meetings.

2.7   Professional Advisers

BANKERS
BABB Bank Plc.
High Street Branch, Guildford
Mr. James Nobody
Tel. 01252 000 555

ACCOUNTANTS
Ivor Gunn and Associates
The Old House, Guildford
Mr. Ivor Gunn
Tel. 01252 000 222

LEGAL ADVISORS
The Little Law Firm
100 High Street, Guildford
Mrs. Jane Wright
Tel. 01252 000 111

NON-EXECUTIVE DIRECTOR
Dr. Abdul Doolittle
Expert Investments Plc.
1 Mayfair, London
Tel. 01202 000 000

2.8   Recruitment of Key Employees

There are no human resources issues as Market Précis will use the well-established British outsourcing firm, EURO BPO Limited. Relying upon their expertise, we shall commence operations with only one employee, the Technical Director.

We shall use our network of accredited freelance agents to create the written content itself. These agents are paid according to work completed according to our contracts of engagement and as self-employed freelancers they are without any overhead, liabilities or expenses.

Market Précis Ltd. ™

2.9 Human Resources & Organisation Chart

The Directors foresee no requirement to employ staff in first year of operations by virtue of the fact that all production and 'back office' functions are outsourced.

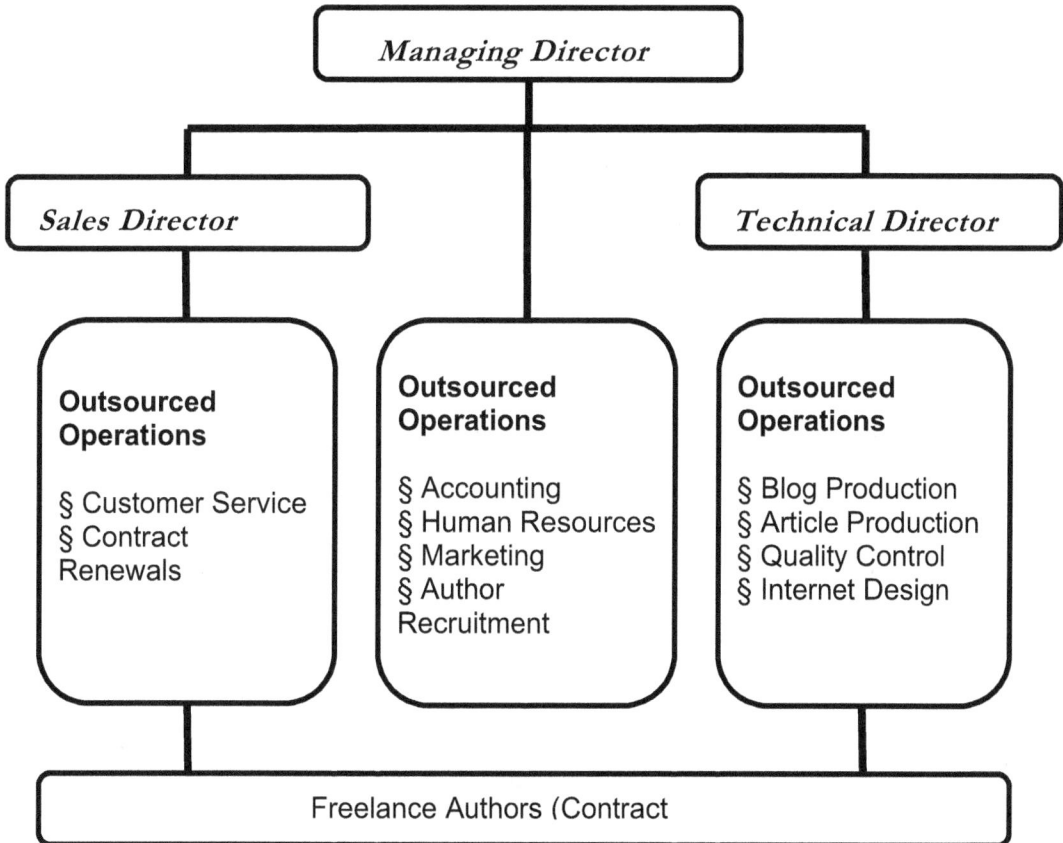

```
                    ┌─────────────────────────┐
                    │   Managing Director      │
                    └─────────────────────────┘
                                 │
         ┌───────────────────────┴───────────────────────┐
┌──────────────────┐                          ┌──────────────────────┐
│  Sales Director  │                          │  Technical Director  │
└──────────────────┘                          └──────────────────────┘
         │                      │                          │
```

Outsourced Operations

§ Customer Service
§ Contract Renewals

Outsourced Operations

§ Accounting
§ Human Resources
§ Marketing
§ Author Recruitment

Outsourced Operations

§ Blog Production
§ Article Production
§ Quality Control
§ Internet Design

Freelance Authors (Contract

Section Three: The Market

3.1 Market Overview

Market Précis occupies a niche within the marketing industry referred to as 'Content Creation', which as an internet marketing industry is approximately twelve years old.

The four vendors in the United Kingdom are not entrenched: only two have been in business for more than five years, while two have been in business for three years. All are expanding quickly as the market shifts from the cottage industry of before.

The impetus for change was due to the major internet search engines, such as Google© changing their software algorithms in 2014 to reflect that website content is now more important than 'key words': only the most 'complete' websites will gain top results. The marketing problem lies with the huge cost of creating this optimised content.

Website managers are struggling to both create content and to broadcast it across multiple channels such as web browsers and social media networks. These costs are crippling both IT and marketing budgets. It is this for which our Content as a Service (CaaS) solution is designed.

Both in the UK and globally, traditional marketing agencies now seek to outsource the production. Market Précis will enter the market as a disruptive force, bringing both leading technology and a markedly lower cost structure to challenge the incumbent providers.

We have identified an immature but growing marketplace into which a new entrant can reasonably expect to challenge the current vendors for a commanding position.

3.2 Market Trends

The market is dynamic and, just as SEO was the buzzword for the past ten years, 'content' is now the new frontier. Key growth factors include the demand for content to be translated into multiple languages, and for the data to be revised and updated constantly.

The analysts *Big Analysts Inc.,* forecast a rapid five-year growth of content creation vendors followed by industry standard consolidation. The lifecycle is indefinite.

Of particular importance is that this technological imperative is now affordable to, and demanded by, the SME sector.

3.3   Demographic, Economic, Cultural & Social Factors

As a business to business provider of marketing services, the primary consideration for Market Précis is that of social factors. In this we see the explosive demand for e-Commerce and overall website presence. In this the demand far outstrips supply, and thus our marketplace is, to all intents and purposes, unlimited.

e-Commerce is the driving force behind the demand for both content and CaaS (Content as a Service), regardless of whether one is in an SME or 'blue chip' corporation. It is a 'must have, especially since 78% of the global population now have mobile phones. The World is a connected place and global corporations demand global marketing.

The thirst for knowledge and service has driven the transition from static web sites towards those with engaging content, irrespective of age, language or location.

Behaviourally, it is the content which creates the bond between the consumer and the operator of the website, and it is this which makes Content Creation such an exciting field: there is an unlimited global marketplace for the specialist.

3.4   The Market Segment

Our niche is firmly targeted at fulfilling the market demand for outsourced textual content of high quality and which is delivered in a manageable form. We shall not compete with vendors offering audio and video since these lie outside of our area of expertise and have entirely different logistical requirements and cost structures.

There are leaders in the field of content creation, and leaders in CaaS software, but Market Précis will be the first to exploit the combination of optimised textual content creation together with a modern delivery mechanism. Combined with our web services model we will have a compelling business proposition upon which we can introduce new technologies.

With four established vendors as noted in (3.1), Market Précis will secure its position by offering unrivalled language options (localisation of content), and through the innovation of renting content as a service, two of our leading differentiators.

3.5   Products & Services

CONTENT CREATION: MPCONTENT ®

Our flagship product. This is the our unique, high quality marketing content. Scalable and flexible, it can cover an unlimited number of vertical market topics. Clients subscribe to content creation services and receive a stream of unique content according to contracted volumes. It's content rental: customisable and re-usable.

WEB PRODUCTS: MPWEB ®

Combining premium content with full automation and implementation of fully customised website Landing Pages. This positions us with the product leaders and reflects the most sophisticated marketing techniques in the Digital Age.

CAAS DELIVERY: MPCAAS ®

The absolute differentiator for Market Précis is our sophisticated application of Content as a Service, enabling marketing departments to be free of the customisation of content for multiple platforms. MPCaaS removes a specific IT challenge from the marketing department.

PROFESSIONAL SERVICES

Market Précis will scale-up to offer the following full range of professional services, including:

- o   Marketing portals with engaged subscribers
- o   Graphics design
- o   Translation from English to any one of 32 languages
- o   Mobile App development
- o   Website design
- o   Management of Google AdWords campaigns
- o   Google AdWords analytics
- o   Search Engine Optimization (SEO

3.6   Risk Factors & Implications

The potential technological risk factors for the Market Précis business model are minimal. The product lifecycle is certainly greater than ten years, and with the maturation of internet search engine technology the industry outlook is stable. Moreover, our core product is 'knowledge', not replaceable by technology.

The primary commercial risk factor is the potential to be undermined on unit production costs, in this case, costs of authoring. The business plan is entirely geared towards the mitigation of this risk. The management approaches include the minimisation of capital outlay, reduced employment costs and the avoidance of debt. Key features include:

- o   Use of outsourcing to eliminate the need for full-time, directly-employed 'back office' staff, coupled with the use of global freelancers under contract for authoring services.
- o   The services are prepaid by the clients for a minimum contract terms. This ensures no opportunity for client debts and transforms the cash flow.
- o   The business uses 'Software as a Service' (SaaS), greatly reducing our start-up costs and enabling instant scalability according to client load.
- o   Our marketing is automatically scaled according to client load, even on a weekly basis.
- o   Our cost of sale is minimalized through the use of digital communications, including VOIP, video and online interaction.
- o   There is no absolute reliance on any single underlying programming architecture or software toolkit/API.
- o   Our subscription model may be imitated but our early market lead will generate a captive audience: clients are reluctant to cancel any subscription as this means they must start with new supplier and build new relationships.

While the Market Précis cost basis has an unassailable advantage in the current market segment, our vertical market focus offers considerable differentiation to our competitors. We shall compete on quality and ease of delivery.

3.7 S.W.O.T. Analysis

Strengths	Weaknesses
• Management have industry experience and strong reputation • Extensive client contacts • Lowest production cost per unit • Product is innovative • Lowest infrastructure costs • Product is a 'must have' for business, not a 'nice to have' • Many ideas for product diversification • Technical superiority in terms of CaaS solution • Strongest multi-lingual output	• Market newcomer – must start with client base of zero • Identified with our past employers • Less funding than the competition • Marketplace still immature and technology could change • No London headquarters could be a potential image problem • Cannot offer video content or other multi-media solutions • No in-house design team for sophisticated artwork creation
Opportunities	Threats
• No other vendor offering such focus upon core vertical industries • Marketplace seeking better customer support • Improved turn-around of media delivery times will differentiate us • Exceptional market demand and not enough suppliers • Competition not using e-Commerce • Delivery of service in many other countries is a wide open market • No other vendor offering data rental / Content as a Service	• Service offering relatively easy to replicate • Competition launching marketing campaign with exceptional funding • Competitors deliver quality products. Difficult to dislodge • Exchange rates could turn adverse and increase production costs by 20% • Business plan success depends on contract renewal rates of >50%

Market Précis Ltd. ™

Section Four: Competition

4.1   Competitive Overview

There are two tiers of competition in the targeted market segment:

Tier One: SME companies which have an average of 26 employees, sophisticated marketing, and a mixture of 'high profile' corporate clients as well as SME clients.

Tier Two: Identified as small teams within larger marketing agencies or the 'cottage industry' of individual authors and consultants. They lack the capacity to deliver the volumes of data demanded by our targeted client base. Many are regarded potential resellers for our solutions.

Market Précis will compete in Tier One. In this segment there are three established firms, all based in London and all of which are privately held limited companies.

Of the Tier One competitors, only ABC Content Limited, has been trading for more than five years. All have high profile corporate clients, including various FTSE 100 corporations and international brand names.

The competitors are all noted for professionalism, quality, reliability and service. Based upon annual returns, all are experiencing annual growth of >30%.

The opportunity for a new market entrant remains positive because the established vendors are burdened with high cost structures, inflexible delivery models, and an overall lack of 'new technology' with which to respond to shifting client demands.

4.2   Competitors & Type of Competition

- ○ ABC Content Limited, London   Direct Competitor
    www.abccontent.com

- ○ 123 Original Content Limited, London   Direct Competitor
    www.123original.com

- ○ eContents Online Limited, London   Direct Competitor
    www.econtentsonline.co.uk

4.3   Competitors Strengths & Weaknesses

Our market research indicates that Market Précis will be positioned in the mid-point in terms of price but with clear differentiators in terms of what we can offer above and beyond the competition.

Vendor Name	Avg. Unit Price	Languages	Caas Capable	Website Services	Subscription Model	Quality Reputation	Turnaround	Vertical Focus?	Number of Staff
ABC Content	£120	12	NO	YES		HIGH	10	Partial	30
123 Original	£65	6	NO	NO		MED	5	Partial	13
eContents	£65	1	NO	NO		MED	5	NO	20
Market Précis	£80	32	YES	YES	YES	(N/A)	5	YES	8

While ABC Content Limited is by far the most established competitor, and with a superb reputation, we can challenge them on both price and speed of turnaround.

The opportunity in the UK marketplace is a simple proposition: the market demand greatly exceeds supply for specialist content creation services.

4.4   Competitive Advantage

We combine low overhead with a unique subscription model to forge long lasting relationships with our client base.

Our technical expertise with CaaS gives us a clear competitive advantage, and an assured six-month head-start in the UK marketplace for combining CaaS with content generation.

Analysis of our pricing model indicates that we can, if required, charge up to 30% less than any of our competitors and still achieve a positive cash flow, with solid revenue and profitability.

Market Précis Ltd.™

Section Five: Sales & marketing

5.1   Sales and Marketing Objectives

Market Précis have developed a comprehensive sales and marketing plan which is available for review.

The initial marketing goal is to create brand awareness. Using a combination of our own content product, social media, Google AdWords and a series of viral media videos our marketing will ensure we appear in the top five results of relevant Google searches and, specifically, that we are 'above the fold'.

The marketing shall transition to conveying our brand and product positioning. We shall combine our value proposition with one of five rotating themes, each supported by a customised campaign. These shall include:

- o   We can deliver the highest quality content.
- o   We understand why tailored content is so important to you
- o   We are focused on your industry
- o   We have the most flexible offering in the marketplace
- o   We know the importance of using the best of emerging web-based marketing techniques

The sales objectives call for generating 30% of revenue from Large Enterprise clients and 40% from SME's. The sales cycle tends to vary from 4 – 12 weeks. Our buyers are marketing directors or 'C' Level.

We shall measure our marketing success on the criteria we know to be proven in our industry:

- o   24 qualified sales presentations per month
- o   12 sales proposals submitted
- o   6 contract negotiations initiated
- o   2 contracts exchanged

Achieving these very reasonable objectives shall assure business success.

5.2 Financial Objectives of Sales & Marketing

The sales and marketing plan is geared entirely towards achieving our core financial objectives:

- ○ Achieve 1st year revenue of £300,000 @ EBIT £30,000
- ○ Achieve 2nd year revenue of £575,000 @ EBIT £125,000
- ○ Achieve 3rd year revenue of £775,000 @ EBIT £200,000

Success for the Market Précis go-to-market business model is based upon achieving four Large Enterprise contracts and 10 SME contracts in FY1.

The business will commence operations with one Large Enterprise and one SME contract in place. We shall then target our efforts on securing one further Large Enterprise sale and three SME sales per quarter, well within industry norms.

The Directors highlight the FY2 growth is based up a subscription contract renewal rate of 50%. This realistic estimate is fully achievable and is based upon industry averages for SaaS contracts.

5.3 Target Markets

Market Précis is a Business to Business vendor. The broad marketplace is typified by any business with a marketing manager and more than 20 employees.

Emphasis upon specific vertical markets lower costs and, since our business rents the data to the client, such concentration lends itself to re-use of data.

Our marketing effort is targeted to four specific verticals:

- ○ Tourism (domestic, European and global)
- ○ Lifestyle (including health, fitness, leisure)
- ○ Information Technology
- ○ Legal

There are many additional vertical markets which are well suited and these represent opportunity for growth and diversification.

5.4 Positioning the Brand

The brand shall be positioned as much more than a mere product set. Our emphasis upon service, delivery and maintenance will position the brand as a differentiated strategic ally: we shall build upon client partnership.

Client surveys highlight the demand for specialists in specific fields. We shall highlight our focus and expertise within the client's exact industry marketplace.

5.5 Pricing

We estimate our pricing to be positioned at the 20% above the market mid-point, noting that the variety of services make this hard to quantify absolutely.

While no other vendor offers a similar delivery model, this is calculated by averaging out the unit cost quoted by the competition. All figures are for a 12-month subscription.

Annual contract rates are as follows:

Product	Per Year
MPContent (Enterprise)	£30,480
MPContent (SME)	£15,240
MPWeb (Enterprise)	£8,000
MPWeb (SME)	£4,000
MPCaaS Service	£2,400
Translation	£0.02 per word

Large Enterprise clients: Includes start-up package of 24 articles and 24 blog pieces, followed by a monthly delivery of 8 articles and 12 blog pieces. Annually, the client receives 120 articles and 168 blog pieces inclusive of graphics and SEO optimisation.

SME clients: Includes start-up package of 12 articles and 12 blog pieces, followed by a monthly delivery of 4 articles and 6 blog pieces. Annually, the client receives 60 articles and 84 blog pieces inclusive of graphics and SEO optimisation.

MPWeb: clients can adjust the timing of the marketing campaigns with the integrated Landing Pages. All data analytics are included as is the design of custom Landing Pages.

5.6   Product Marketing & Promotion

QUALITY PROPOSITION

Even the most dedicated marketing professional cannot create a comparable flow of original writing as offered by a team of experts. For our target market, The Market Précis' quality proposition is absolute: quality content requires diversification of message, style and thought.

VALUE PROPOSITION

A 'Large Enterprise' client receives 120 articles and 168 blog pieces within their twelve-month subscription, all with graphics and full SEO optimisation. The industry average for authoring an article is 12 hours, and 4 hours for a blog. Thus, In-house creation requires 214 days of manpower excluding the time required for locating or creating artwork, third-party proofing etc.

Regardless of the size of client, our significant value proposition is that our service saves a London based firm approximately 50% compared to the cost of using a full time employee, and 30% for a provincial firm.

PROMOTION

The Directors of Market Précis have a highly innovative website design which is nearing completion. Behind this we will be exploiting our own products and services to the full, with more than 200 pages of original content.

A Google AdWords campaign will be launched. This will combine Search Engine Optimisation techniques with a business to business email marketing campaign inviting clients to our in-house designed Landing Pages. Clients will then be presented with appropriate Calls to Action. For example, subscribe (with only email address) to receive an instant download of one of three eBooks, or to attend a seminar or to receive market information.

Other marketing initiatives will follow using the same techniques, including:

- ○ Producing specific White Papers for our vertical markets
- ○ Hosting monthly seminars in the form of 'working lunches'
- ○ Publishing an industry news feed in the form of a blog on the main website

5.7 Service

Our service strategy hinges on providing our clients with exemplary quality original content, carefully proofed, diligently translated, and formatted for delivery according to the Service Level Agreement.

We have designed and testing a robust quality assurance model which uses human review and editing combined with advanced publishing software techniques to ensure accuracy on all fronts and to prevent plagiarism.

5.8 Distribution Channels

Our first year of operations will be exclusively through direct sales.

In our second year we will be seeking partnerships with mainstream marketing agencies through whom we can offer our content for resale.

5.9 Key Suppliers

Supplier	Payment Terms
EURO BPO Ltd., United Kingdom *Outsourced staffing services for marketing, quality control, IT, finance, call handling*	Payment in advance, monthly
Contentmagic GmbH, Germany *Supplier of core software, the CaaS API*	Payment in advance, monthly
Internet Provider Ltd., United Kingdom *Web hosting & data centres*	Net 30 / £1,000 credit limit

5.10 Customers

Client Name: Big Hotel Group Plc., London

Contract Value: £70,560

Contract Term:12 months

During our 12-month R&D process, Market Précis piloted a 'proof of concept' with Big Hotel Group Plc., London, who have issued a contract conditional upon successful start-up.

> **"** ... *the value of this initial contract is £64,000, with planned expansion to their European operations ...*

This chain of 32 boutique hotels is focussed on the leisure tourism sector and their marketing need is for each location to be supported by core-content articles translated into five languages, with an enhanced series of blog pieces to support both the localised message and the corporate message.

Starting with a standard 12 months' contract term, the value of this initial contract is £64,000, with planned expansion to their European operations to follow in Q4.

In addition to the above, Market Précis have developed a sales pipeline which includes one FTSE 100 corporation, 3 'Large Enterprise' and 6 SME clients, the majority of which operate in our core verticals of tourism and leisure.

Market Précis Ltd.™

Section Six: Operations

6.1   Operating Plan

Facilities

No office facilities are required for FY1. The business shall make use of an outsourcing agency which offers client meeting facilities within the scope of the service contract. Routine client conferences will be held at the outsourced offices, reached by short flight within Europe.

Staffing

The use of a Business Process Outsourcing agency ensures the business has its own team of selected and dedicated staff. They are fully tasked with support to Market Précis. This eliminates are Human Resources tasks, as well as any overheads such employer contributions, benefits etc. The business shall commence with a total of five contracted staff members.

Suppliers

Arrangements are in place with the three primary suppliers, with only the contract for the Business Process Outsourcing to be concluded.

Inventory

The business will not require any inventory, except for the creation of a core body of work which shall be available for use by our clients. This is reported within the start-up costs.

Equipment

Although aspects of the business are IT systems intensive, the network infrastructure is outsourced to our internet / web hosting provider.

Process

The sales team complete a detailed on-line needs analysis with the client. This forms the project specification and defines, for example, exactly what articles are required, their style, format, audience needs, graphics specifications – indeed more than sixty parameters in total.

The client initiates a contract through an online interface to which the client can also upload their purchase order. A formal contract is generated automatically.

The contract requires a deposit of 50% of the total contract value, with the balance being invoiced as eleven monthly instalments. This approach models the proven Software as a Service (SaaS) approach and it is within the expertise of the Directors.

After payment the governing Service Level Agreement defines the delivery of the first tranche of content (articles and blogs). These are created by our team of freelancers who work under contract. Their production requirements are also governed by an SLA.

The articles and blogs are received by the outsourced Quality Assurance manager who reviews, approves or rejects, and edits. If the contract stipulates graphics creation, there is a sub-loop while it is completed by the outsourced graphics designer.

The 'packet' is passed to management for acceptance, and then uploaded to the client either by a smart transfer protocol or via the Market Précis MPCaaS solution.

The process is then in a contract maintenance phase and delivery continues weekly until the conclusion of the contract.

6.2   Technical Overview

The technology upon which our CaaS solution relies is the Software Developers' Toolkit (SDK) from ContentMagic in Germany. This provides us with the means to deliver our content in Extensible Mark-up Language (XML) to corporate marketing departments for instantaneous re-structuring and branding according to their presentation demands (such as platform).

For an extended review of this technology, we refer you to the White Paper detailed in the appendix.

Market Précis Ltd.™

6.3 Government Regulation

There are no applicable government regulations with respect to the product offering.

6.4 Equipment, Technology, R&D

There are no anticipated requirements for specialist equipment, technology or further R&D until Year 2.

6.5 Environmental Considerations

There are no applicable environmental considerations since the entire product creation, marketing and delivery is 100% online.

6.6 Action Plan and Timetable

The Market Précis 20 Week Action Plan is detailed in the Gantt Chart below. This details the major milestones and is taken from our master Action Plan.

There is a 12-week build-up to soft 'go live' (indicated by the vertical red line), and by week 16 all staff will be fully trained with fully tested production, quality control, delivery and customer service procedures and protocols in place.

Week	1	2	3	4	5	6	7	8	9	10	11	12	13	14	15	16	17	18	19	20

Management
Legal: Finalise trademarks
Accounting: tax approvals
Outsourcing: Contract?

Marketing
Website design testing
Create social media presence
AdWords campaign
PR company to start
Create internal content

Staffing
Advertise for freelancers
Freelancer agreements
Outsourcing training

Sales
Secure 1st contracts
Build pipeline

Section Seven: Financials

FY 1

Product Receipts	1	2	3	4	5	6	7	8	9	10	11	12
MPContent (ENT)	15,240	1,385	1,385	16,625	2,770	2,770	2,770	18,010	4,155	4,155	4,155	19,395
MPContent (SME)	7,620	8,313	8,313	1,386	16,626	8,313	10,392	8,313	18,705	8,313	12,471	5,544
MPWeb (ENT)	8,000			8,000				8,000				8,000
MPWeb (SME)	4,000		4,000		8,000		4,000		8,000		4,000	
MPCaaS				2,400			2,400			2,400		
Professional Svcs		3,000		3,000		3,000		3,000		3,000		3,000
Contract Extension												
Total Receipts	34,860	12,698	13,698	31,411	27,396	14,083	19,562	37,323	30,860	17,868	20,626	35,939

Payments	1	2	3	4	5	6	7	8	9	10	11	12
Cash purchases	300	300	300	300	300	300	300	300	300	300	300	300
Pmts. to creditors												
Salaries	3,000	3,000	3,000	3,000	3,000	3,000	3,000	3,000	3,000	3,000	3,000	3,000
Wages	4,000	4,000	4,000	4,000	4,000	4,000	6,000	6,000	6,000	6,000	6,000	6,000
Accounts/HR	1,000	1,000	1,000	1,000	1,000	1,000	1,000	1,000	1,000	1,000	1,000	1,000
Rent												
Utilities												
Insurance	500											
Travel	2,400	2,400	2,400	2,400	2,400	2,400	3,600	3,600	3,600	3,600	3,600	3,600
Telephone	180	180	180	180	180	180	180	180	180	180	180	180
IT spend	300	300	300	300	300	300	300	300	300	300	300	300
Office supplies	100	100	100	100	100	100	100	100	100	100	100	100
Advertising												
Marketing	3,000	3,000	3,000	3,000	3,000	3,000	3,000	3,000	3,000	3,000	3,000	3,000
Professional fees												1,000
Bank charges												
Owner's drawings	6,000	6,000	6,000	6,000	6,000	6,000	6,000	6,000	6,000	6,000	6,000	6,000
Loan repayments												
Tax payments												
Capital purchases												
Total Payments	20,780	20,280	20,280	20,280	20,280	20,280	23,480	23,480	23,480	23,480	23,480	24,480

	1	2	3	4	5	6	7	8	9	10	11	12
Profit (Loss)	14,080	-7,582	-6,582	11,131	7,116	-6,197	-3,918	13,843	7,380	-5,612	-2,854	11,459
Cash Flow (Deficit)	94,080	86,498	79,916	91,047	98,163	91,966	88,048	101,891	109,271	103,659	100,805	112,264

Market Précis Ltd.™

7.1 FY1: Revenue & Expense Forecast

NOTE: Opening cash balance of £80,000. Revenue is allocated in the month the product or service is delivered.

	FY 1				FY 2				FY 3			
Product Receipts	Q1	Q2	Q3	Q4	Q1	Q2	Q3	Q4	Q1	Q2	Q3	Q4
MPContent (ENT)	18,010	22,165	24,935	27,705	23,413	28,815	32,416	36,017	30,437	37,459	29,713	46,821
MPContent (SME)	24,246	26,325	37,410	26,328	31,520	34,223	48,633	34,226	40,976	44,489	63,223	44,494
MPWeb (ENT)	8,000	8,000	8,000	8,000	10,400	10,400	10,400	10,400	13,520	13,520	13,520	13,520
MPWeb (SME)	8,000	8,000	12,000	4,000	10,400	10,400	15,600	5,200	13,520	13,520	20,280	6,760
MPCaaS	0	2,400	2,400	2,400	2,400	3,120	3,120	3,120	3,120	4,056	4,056	4,056
Professional Svcs	3,000	6,000	3,000	6,000	3,900	7,800	3,900	7,800	5,070	5,070	5,070	10,140
Contract Extension	0	0	0	0	41,017	47,378	57,034	48,381	61,526	71,068	85,552	72,572
Total Receipts	61,256	72,890	87,745	74,433	123,050	142,135	171,103	145,144	168,169	189,182	221,414	198,364
Payments	Q1	Q2	Q3	Q4	Q1	Q2	Q3	Q4	Q1	Q2	Q3	Q4
Cash purchases	900	900	900	900	900	900	900	900	900	900	900	900
Payments to creditors	0	0	0	0	0	0	0	0	0	0	0	0
Salaries (Outsourced)	9,000	9,000	9,000	9,000	24,000	24,000	24,000	24,000	36,000	36,000	36,000	36,000
Wages (Freelancers)	12,000	12,000	18,000	18,000	24,000	24,000	30,000	30,000	36,000	36,000	42,000	42,000
Payroll/accounts/HR	3,000	3,000	3,000	3,000	3,000	3,000	3,000	3,000	3,000	3,000	3,000	3,000
Rent	0	0	0	0	0	0	0	0	0	0	0	0
Utilities	0	0	0	0	0	0	0	0	0	0	0	0
Insurance	500	0	0	0	500	0	0	0	500	0	0	0
Travel	7,200	7,200	10,800	10,800	10,800	10,800	10,800	10,800	10,800	10,800	10,800	10,800
Telephone	540	540	540	540	540	540	540	540	540	540	540	540
IT spend	900	900	900	900	900	900	900	900	900	900	900	900
Office supplies	300	300	300	300	600	600	600	600	900	900	900	900
Advertising	0	0	0	0	0	0	0	0	0	0	0	0
Marketing/promotion	9,000	9,000	9,000	9,000	9,000	9,000	9,000	9,000	9,000	9,000	9,000	9,000
Professional fees	0	0	0	1,000	0	0	0	1,000	0	0	0	1,000
Bank charges	0	0	0	0	0	0	0	0	0	0	0	0
Owner's drawings	18,000	18,000	18,000	18,000	36,000	36,000	36,000	36,000	45,000	45,000	45,000	45,000
Loan repayments	0	0	0	0	0	0	0	0	0	0	0	0
Tax payments	0	0	0	0	0	0	0	0	0	0	0	0
Capital purchases	0	0	0	0	0	0	0	0	0	0	0	0
Total Payments	61,340	60,840	70,440	71,440	110,240	109,740	115,740	116,740	143,540	143,040	149,040	150,040
Profit (Loss)	-84	12,050	17,305	2,993	12,810	32,395	55,363	28,404	24,629	46,142	72,374	48,324
Cash Flow(Deficit)	79,916	91,966	109,271	112,264	125,074	157,469	212,831	241,235	265,864	312,006	384,380	432,704

7.2 FY1 - 3: Revenue & Expense Forecast

NOTE: Opening cash balance of £80,000. Revenue is allocated in the month the product or service is delivered.

7.3 Graphical P&L Forecasts (FY 1 & FY 1-3)

P&L FY 1 (Monthly)

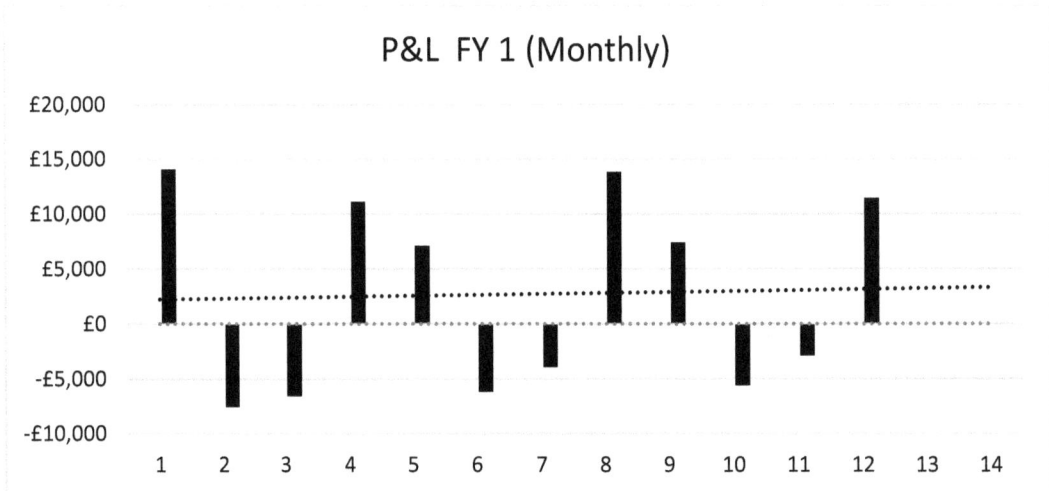

P&L FY 1 - 3 (Quarterly)

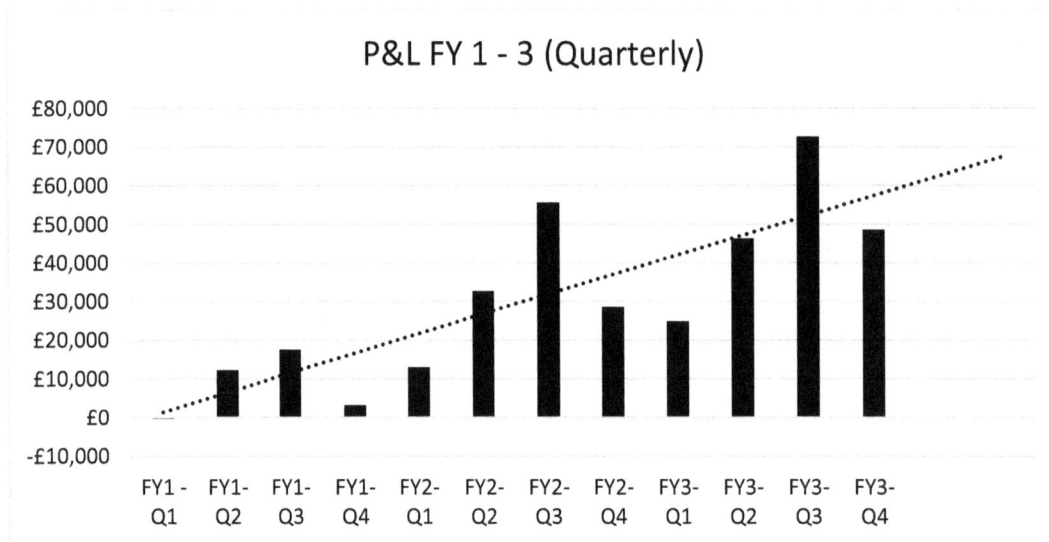

Market Précis Ltd.™

7.4 Graphical Cash Flow Forecasts (FY1 & FY1-3)

Cash Flow FY 1 (Monthly)
(opening cash balance of £80,000)

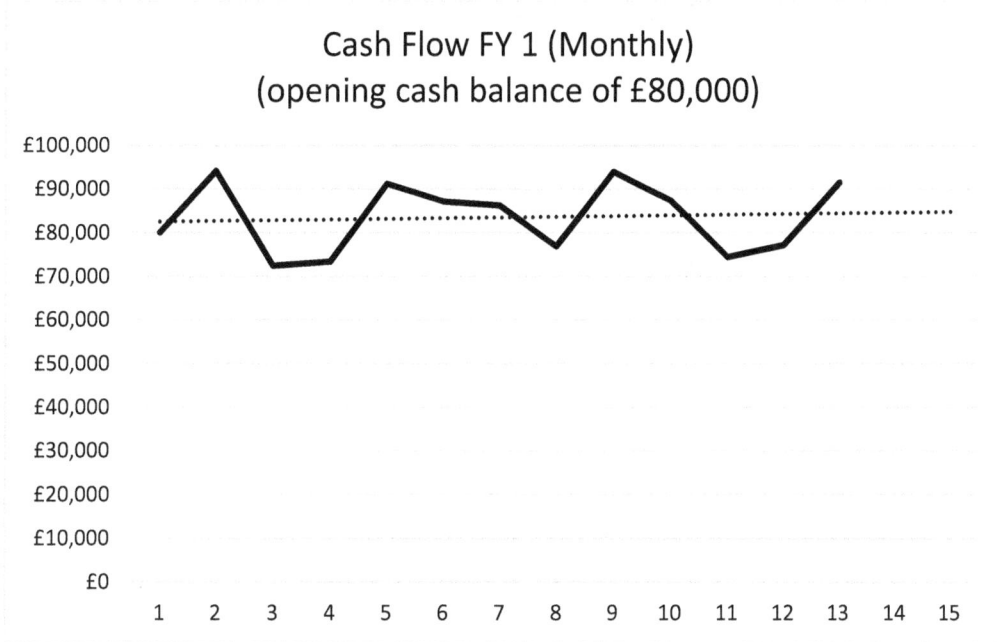

Cash Flow FY 1-3 (Quarterly)
(opening cash balance of £80,000)

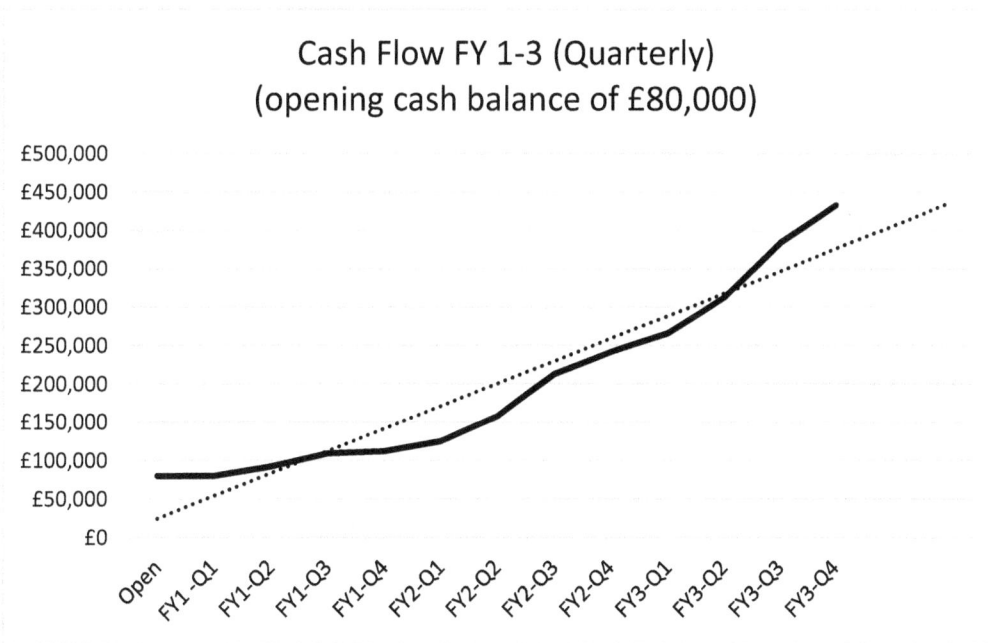

7.5 Source of Revenue by Product or Service

FY 1 Revenue by Product or Service

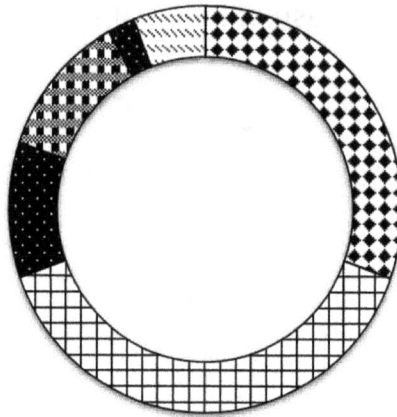

- ⊞ MPContent (ENT) ☐ MPContent (SME) ■ MPWeb (ENT) ▣ MPWeb (SME)
- ■ MPCaaS ☐ Professional Svcs ■ Contract Extension

FY 1-3 Revenue by Product or Service

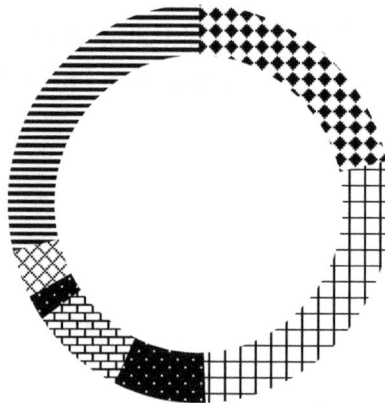

- ⠒ MPContent (ENT) + MPContent (SME) ■ MPWeb (ENT) ⊤ MPWeb (SME)
- ■ MPCaaS ⤢ Professional Svcs = Contract Extension

Note the impact of service contract renewals following FY1. This is the key to achievable growth rates.

Market Précis Ltd.™

7.6 Financial Summary

	FY 1	FY 2	FY 3
Revenue	£296,324	£581,431	£777,129
Expense	£264,060	£452,460	£585,660
P/L (EBIT)	£32,264	£128,971	£191,469

3 Year P/L (EBIT)	£352,704
Initial Investment	£120,000
3 Year ROI	294%

Section Eight: Appendix

8.1 Supporting Documents

8.1   Certificate of Incorporation

8.2   Shareholders Agreement

8.3   Trademark Certificate

8.4   HMRC Tax Approval Certificate (special schemes)

8.5   Non-disclosure Agreement

8.6   Detailed Action Plan (Gantt Chart)

8.2 Additional Resources

www.ingramcontent.com/pod-product-compliance
Lightning Source LLC
Chambersburg PA
CBHW061127210326
41518CB00034B/2543